AF594738

Comin' 'Round

(Selected Writings)

Comin' 'Round

(Selected Writings)

James Sherry

chax 2025

ISBN 978-1-946104-55-7

Library of Congress Card Number: 2024946318

First Edition First Printing by Chax Press, Tucson

Chax Press is supported by individual donors, and by the Arts Foundation for Tucson and Southern Arizona, the Arizona Commission on the Arts, and the Tucson Foundations. We hope you will decide to support Chax, and you may visit our web site at chax.org to find out more about us and to make a contribution to our work in publishing, literary and book arts education, and public presentations of literary and artistic matters.

Special thanks to our Creative Arts Director Cynthia Miller, and to our inspiring Board of Directors, for their work on behalf of Chax Press. Our directors are

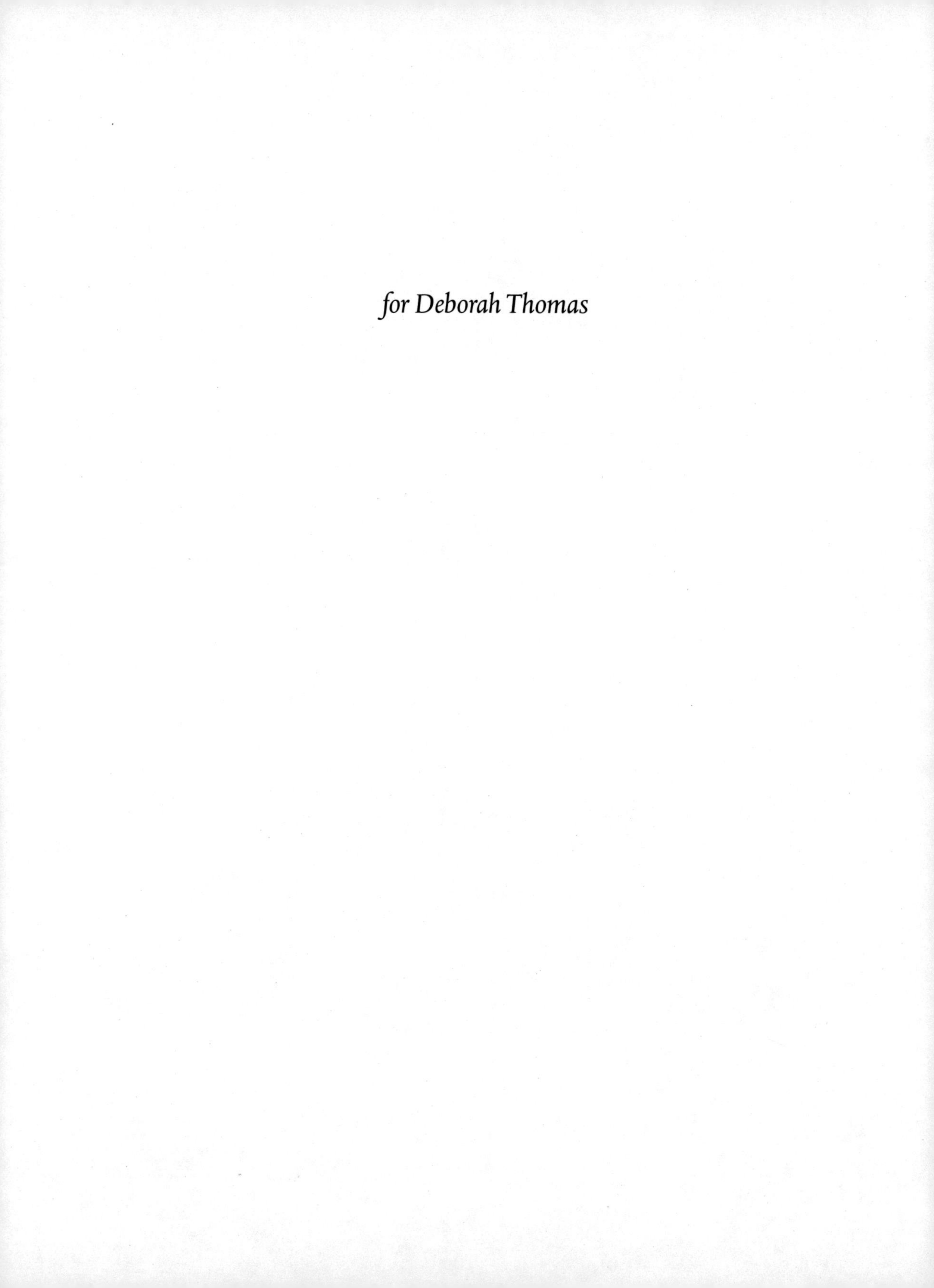

for Deborah Thomas

Contents

Lazy Sonnets

1970-1972

To the Reader

O you who like to nap each afternoon,
before you start to saw the log,
remember I'm the laziest.
I write everything from sleep's threshold—love,
politics, nature, paradise—and in
lazy numbers, lazy rhyme,
composed these lines on my back. I
claim work's laziness, a way to face
away from oblivion, and lying
down martyrdom. I'm not carried away
by dreams or jumping up to wave a flag,
but hover in between these sheets, my eyes on you
to best be seen. Listen.

Idyll

Maybe I don't understand my own mind,
but when I try to find some reasons why
I'm always dozing, thoughts flock around, eager
to be the one I choose; so I can't.
If I do pick one, the others intrude.
If I catch one by the neck, it babbles
to be returned. And if by inertia
or impetus beyond control I'm carried
beyond them to where I know their names,
I can't think; I don't know how I got here;
I don't remember really what happened.
It's as if I slept and dreamed I'd know
why I slept when I woke up.

Platonic Laziness

Face in pillow at verge of day,
perfectly restrained I hear the busses.
They do not make me nervous. I obey
another urge than rushing to the office.
I have but one ambition—Repose.
Suspending animation is my quest . . .
Let's say I'm lazy. Let me yawn, stretch, doze,
but not get up, not sleep deep in my nest.
My face is crushed flat and flushed, and my lips nurse.
As I approach ideal languorousness,
my random thoughts recline along this verse.
But I can't mail ms. to your address,
since even model laziness has a hitch.
Although I ache and itch, I must not budge.

Devotee

O you little pebbles on which my temple rests,
you wake my yearning for Aergia
and her gummy-eyed attendant's laziness.
I bow my head and do nothing alone
and in darkness I serve. Nothing can keep
me up. And through all I hear far thumping;
strange night bodies shuffle. Draft on my head.
I cover up. Music muffled by swathed
columns. Players under water flicker.
I see light. Is this my torch I hold?
I follow. We're all novices, dancing.
I imitate the steps, abasing myself,
accepting stumbling giving rise to power.
All discomfort, all opinions I turn over.

Statics

I focus horizontally, the plane
I'm inclined to rely on. But there's
more than one position between getting
into bed and getting out. Lying down's
necessity for sick ones, good luck
for tired ones, pleasure for sluggards,
the normal state of the intellect,
the vocation of prostitutes, employment
for the poet, the salvation of Rip
van Winkle, and custom in Miami Beach.
There are many many ways of being prone:
But how I further sleep or wake you up,
I wouldn't say even if I could.
You'd have to change at once or close this book.

The Source

Exploring words to find the source of Laziness,
while tributaries enter from surrounding hills,
I seek the mainstream whose loving flows
washed away the toothpicks propping up my lids,
returning me to a natural state.
When I trekked upstream, my love diverged
from sleep. Scrambling up scree slopes and sheer cliffs
pitons point to peril in this languorous
silence surrounding. I approach her spring. Breasts
float in white tub. I ask her, "Have your wiles caused
my downfall. Have you kept me from duty, drained
my strength." After a pause she answers, "You know that."

Sloth

My sloth is two-toed and hangs upside down,
diverting boredom with this novelty
or crawling to maintain my camouflage
to a certain finish, gumming my greens.
I can ignore all but the basic
Necessities—breathing, eating, sleeping.
My well-oiled joints ease me up the tree. Thumbs
fire, wheels, writing, iron are conveniences
from my point of view. I like big soft leaves,
papaya, jungly atmosphere, mango,
tango, poolside drinks. Why push upward,
pressing fragile principle? All must succumb:
Head, shoulders, rubber double over.
What strength to stand erect and flex.

Entropy

I don't build cities; nature tears them down.
I don't bow and whisper, seeking favors,
claiming nature likes all who like her
give in. I don't bother to get up.
If my words exactly matched reality,
if I could write a bed, you'd give up reading.
So I stand between you and the bed.
If my prosody exactly matched this form,
you'd give up and read old sonnets. Thinking
what I might say makes me yawn. Space spins,
breathes with awful presence as if aware.
And I have a suspicion as I lie here
in the dark, afraid, suppressing my breath,
as I cry who's there, another cries who's there.

Dialectical Laziness

Dante says, "Nature, disposed to love, creates
Love king." But Love disposed of nature, when,
as figurehead, his subjects and inventions run amuck,
destroying all indifferently: then Love's deposed.
As tyrant they must step on men or step down;
with the same result (Laziness keeps him
from doing his work), lovers sigh oppressed.
Love is irritated matter (after Mann).
Naturally, we're grumpy when awakened;
the longer slaves, the more selfish when we
rise up, like Israel. We can't see normally
how Love distorts us, but by breath note
how every government functions naturally,
how snorting turns to snores. Sleep resigns supreme.

True Love

after John Wilmot

My past life isn't mine anymore.
The hours that dragged by are gone.
Even the endless chase scenes
my dreams labored through recede
among distorted memories.
The future hasn't happened yet.
How can I give what isn't mine?
The present moment's all I have
and that as it arrives, you see,
you suffer until you say when.
Don't tell me I'm ignoring you
or think sometimes of other loves.
That I'm awake and with you for
this minute is a miracle.

Land of Nod

Why, once tucked in, did you get out of bed?
I wanted you to feel at home, but now,
since you can't take part in my favorite comfort,
the poet's poor host to scientific mind
and feeds from his guest, banqueting on slow
experiment that several generations
in communication take to complete.
But is it too difficult to rest assured
or has waking also been elusive?
When you didn't return, I pictured you,
sand weighing down your shoes, head nodding ....
Well, Nantucket Sound's good water for it,
Buzzard's Bay also. But that's the laziest
solitude, where art and science meet,
the slothful and the wrathful solo flights.

Scrap

Not much energy today, don't waste it.
These are not the golden days of plenty
for a few. The time that was predicted
has arrived: worst fears materialize
and what we have as much has us. The more
meek open cans the harder chewing is.
Machines haven't usurped us, don't despair.
They've made those who don't serve them extra
in lazy man's paradise: Do less, get more.
And when death comes, invite them in, give them a beer.
It's not smart to offend high officials.
What can spare parts do but lie still, planning
how they'll do their jobs when the stars break down?

Retirement

Let saplings ease me into this dark pool,
so while bark fissures and deepens and girth
grows soft, shot full of worms, flexible
cambiums will support my seasoned bulk
and hold me up, though storms tear at my roots
and lightning splinters my trunk. They'll let me
down gently through startled cronies' boughs,
slowing as I crash past trunks, falling
as in dreams past root and moss. I crack down
gracefully, past cliffs I've overhung since
first my acorn shot sprouts into space,
until top twigs flick the surface fondly,
and I gaze into the depths. How proud I am
suspended here on healthy progeny.

Utopia

I yawn alone, a no-man of politics,
society's idle wheel, and loaf along;
but if all my friends came with their friends
and they said, get up, we've important jobs;
or if emissaries came with patents
saying, now get up, your friends ask your help
in dispelling illusions and building
a clear-eyed, friendly civilization.
We work without pay; there's plenty of food
for all but leaders, who will get the least,
a plate of vegetables and a hard cot,
for their chance to be powerful; they will be;
clean factories will produce nice machines;
laziness would be justified by consensus.

Prospect

Men's work sends them sooner to the grave.
Women stumble on their gaudy shoes.
Children, satisfied with their toys, grow thin
on indoor pleasures. I imagine
I'm a mummy, wrapped in linen. In my veins
secret ingredients have slowed my decay.
But deep in Lake Nasser, never having
learned to swim, I find a new enemy.
I heard men tapping once outside my crypt.
I bit my crumbling lip, a trifle coy,
safe with my Anubis, no matter how long.
I should rise and let them see my profile,
then turn. They gape and flee my awesome presence,
Osiris, reborn reclining youth.

Morning

for Tamas Guna

In this still, decrepit air my bedroom
is filled with dust hangs in the sun's ray
and knots when I, from time to time, scratch,
although I'd rather not move, longing
for the past that all things remind me of.
This is the drone of my ten o'clock dawn
making melody to drown creaks that joint
and springs intruded on the broken edge
of somnambulance. Finding myself
at the dusty window ledge, dusts on each eyelash
eclipse the sun. I blink, a flutter of shadow.
My profile angles down. Caffeine visionary.
Purity and action are illusions.
The blacktop drive curves upward, peaked roof wind vane.

Red Star

Retroactively for the Deep Sea Fishermen's Union

The red Star chugs toward a distant spot
where clouds have parted and the sea turned white.
But when fishing boat enters the light
where work for fishermen should be brighter,
it's not illuminated. It disappears.
Resolutely gliding across that plane,
I wonder if men inside the wheelhouse fear
the cold deep more than bankrupt pension funds.
I shouldn't think so much about money
or other material manifestations.
But as their ship passes into the dark,
visible again, and zips onward,
and as by law their ship shrinks, I wonder
who weighs success by safety, who by fish?

Ambivalence

Can I, hug the earth and sleep on it,
drugged, drunken, to forget pain and sickness,
leaning on resources to support the weight
of idleness? Can I start up, red gleam
in eye and stalk off to war with my soul,
slow gait, low voice, measured diction,
condescending to continue, abrupt,
wry, willing each fiber to go on
and when leisure comes, luxuriating?
O either is okay. O anything,
but tossing between fire and water,
nutant, mutant, trying to be both and
neither, forever thrashing between cradle
and grave, undecided which way to go.

Siesta

Lymphatism ballasted my ganglia
for years. Naps kept me from tipping over.
But what sustained threatens to drown me daily,
sad fact for a ship rigged in a bottle.
My muscles feel like a Chinese string game,
played in spastic fingers. Flexing them
to pull through would be knots, I stiffen,
twitch. A jumble of fantastic threads.
I linger here in twilight dizziness,
gaping at these thoughts, both tattered having passed
through many minds. But when I do do something,
I allow myself a rest. I'm not bored
with dreaming. I clasp hands behind my head,
pride, gone. Blue flies fizzle through my brain.

Lazy Susan

I look forward anxiously to bedtime,
to warming sheets empty days have dampened,
then losing myself. One minute I'm awake
tied up by worries. (Aren't you ashamed
of your morbid interest in my life?)
Minutes later I might start awake, not
knowing where I am or when, heart beating
madly from glorious deeds. What happens
in between those ticks? I want to stay aware
while falling asleep, while feeling spreads
from head to loin, everywhere, while thoughts form
colored images that float up, spin and sink
so fast they revolve backward, spokes glinting
promises of what comes next, and end waked up.

Ambition

for Kenko

Why don't I conform to propriety
and custom to be (finally) free of them?
Why has my life no goals to shuttle between,
scoring one for void now one for the earth?
My nest rocks with daylight. I wake expecting.
I open my mouth wide, wide. What do I get?
Captured by outside pleasures, joking turns
to quarrels, now resentful, now morbid,
in constant turmoil courting insanity,
calculations of advantage intrude.
Intoxication added to delusion,
worms have more control of what's in their mouths.
I am happiest when I have nothing
to distract me and am completely alone.

Alms

All who adhere to natural indifference
should hear me, all who might like to see life
better than before, but if views worsen,
won't mind much, since they know any effort
can't be directed to its object surely,
and would deplore the carnage of misfire.
All who watch murders, appalled by violence,
witness rape and vow to control their passions,
all who know that nature knows the fitter best,
I call on you to save me.
If each throws me a line and I live,
I'll weave a cradle of indifference for mankind.
And I promise no thanks, no tears.
I'll go my way and forget you.

The Stretch

I can often be found rubbing swollen lids
with hand heels to erase what popped from nowhere,
making eyes redder and sore, focusing,
squinting to see something exist, simply
be on the table. I have a hard time.
Subliming my bedclothes gives me pleasure,
but at what degree of lassitude. I
don't care. "Qu 'ils me laissent rentier."
I want to be free of responsibility,
to move with ease, unseen through diversity,
to oscillate gently from sleep to wakefulness
and not disturb the rest or have to explain
the truth I see beyond polemics, how
only the idle receive revelation.

Bedtime

from Coleridge

It may be lethargy, when I derive
what humans are essentially, what can't
be changed no matter what the creed or structure
of society from sleepy reveries.
Now ambition is frustration's residue
and laziness excess of energies.
So let me lie; and although everyone
tries to wake me up, I sleep as if dead
and thereby do not panic or seek vain jobs.
So will I plump up my pillows, alter them
until they sag. Blankets will be my sky
and no prayer fly up but implores for all
a heartfelt good night and pleasant dreams.

Part Songs

1976-1977

SHE'LL BE COMIN' 'ROUND

She'll be comin' 'round the mountain when the shell sometimes is empty.
She'll be comin' sometimes and the shell is an evasion,
when she comes around the mountain
to put in an appearance;
and this is the introduction we're all trying' to come 'round to.

She'll be drivin' six white and well-bred young mares.
She'll be tryin' to be comin', when one of the horses slips on a curve,
but the traces hold her up
like a beautiful horse about to describe
the great vehicle she'll conduct, when she comes.

And we'll all go out to meet her when the well is dry and cracked
and the water is too neutral to hold
even a chance encounter when we're trying to be comin'
and breathe too much or that's what I
heard when tryin' too hard to meet her, when she comes.

And we'll all have chicken and dumplings in a context
of the human shell, water in the trough,
the gopher holes, how hot leather is in the desert mining town
except to the horses,
when she comes.

DRAWING

for Bob Routch

I.

Fingers tremble over the belly
in whose round lurk the tangled brass
dragons curling up your leg
as you sit between two corpulent
men in overcoats, tickling the curve
of your calf and the circular
cloaca and the spit key.

II.

Call with zephyrs; puff your cheeks o'er curling crests.
Make men war, maids to marry, hounds to hunt
all through alloy, conch and horn; make ships heel to blue.
Though bitter clouds and fatigue appall, you
will not flag; your gleaming pennant cracks.

III.

What is it breathes
   out the mouth,
   through elbows and floodlights stars,
mounting by keys
      the tortuous route
  to the gentling hand,
  to the bell and ear?

What is it breathes
  where cat laps a pool of black
  and where it gets vent
filtering upward
      in a flood of fruit
  through bone and allegro,
  even unto rest?

DRAWING ON COWELL

plick a click track
George Jorge he a
6 1/3 + all
th'the be few an'
to fee the slot.
about time sez fats;
U R gew piano,
pee pee and pee ess a dub
for the queen pluckt ball.

we fey a mute so lolly rebop
yet cue a only thin.
link about is the name
sd. plat w'gad a loop dee la bu'lone
as dense as hair combed over,
labe a rout too loose,
placut time an sup
er car burr ate her ha the loose
wound onde oct half gave please
unter all a flue a spit strin grow
send strand air ope a new a a a:
solo second an have

DRAWING ON STRAUSS

High, yeah, upon yon crag I clung
for want and stung accordingly.
I say "rocketeers" and then silence.
Railroad tracks my pretty
and dizzier than thou art few be.
It is after dinner as usual. Plaster words hang over the high school set.
These immobile,
statuesque women have bilateral breasts and that much suspense is hard to in
fresco. What is the you can't grasp here,
glories the merchant class
imagined man without concert could gain slip away.

Her love is gone and tokens rattle in the drawing room,
where they were and would were
were not followed by this, which is as good at being
itself as any. No loss of what was past.
It's there, relegated and waiting on what
preceded it, but all the while fore and aft
being the length it cannot be otherwise than.
Lost hours were those in regret.

Moving up to Sunday then no; no day but coronation
of the lost Hohenstaufen prince back from China
where he quelled the opium feud with sword, eye
and thoughts of home and empire to be cherished
after Herculean tasks were taken to the hearts
of his journalism-beleaguered countrymen.
How dreams of golden youth become him.
How stories may be told for generations
to a continually avid ear around the hearth.
May be. The image of o let down your hair laughs along
the years where arpeggios disappear in Tiepolo clouds
and sage men try to fathom what they cannot see or hear or taste.

DRAWING ON RECORDED *L'HISTOIRE*

Long shoelaces tree the in-touch networks.
I drag hearing of/ w/ ears
about a condition. Later,
we dined into a worn shoe—
adobe, cane, sticks and stone, the pard,
the fleece, the cannéd been, the lewd pun,

About the fifth rough:
breasts give milk, balls that bounce—
It's me. Once too much.
Program : feelings to survive.
There is no little while later.
Under the bivouac: discontent, modest in ascribing,
tangent if you can will. I can tell you today
what more was along the road : a black pot

You want?
Town section, patties and smoke,
colored cloth, haggle 'n' roll,
once upon a where hair parts:
And after in the stalls
and countless errors, I need.
Let them all be true. Her money settled
on the window ledge, the angle, lost to have,
rich with ardor. Youths always passed.
Hirsute and mud full of glass pranks
might have been. Through the devil's mud
that prepares us for what if;
half of leisure is starvation— a kill, a eat,
a kingdom someone had and then had had. Later we meet
on a dark stair. Treasure may be had and thoughts, but no rest.
What you may want is lost— not to want, not
to have, not to while, when we unearthed. Your
strangest complication is what we have, have had,
would have had, yourself incorrigible, wandering in a suite:

Wonderful vessels, to wash them and shine
in ermine: might have washed day, a stele: rights
of the empty canteen. Fortune ripe into dance, spoke yes
of please, but avoid that room where the track wound in spite of.
The greater the lost the older the grand ball the…
his vision drizzled down
the vertigo

Harsh rebate, solo, and after later came.
This sort of time is tense, blood-stiff cloth.
Home and resolution: Dew Drop Inn : Terminal Hotel.
Fellow met again to use up person.
The room empty, but the eats of mull, the steaks
of state. We trust on a lip, try to genie perfume back in.
What cannot be denied your strength is.
The gold prop gone, let separation off-course charm terror.

DRAWING ON MUSICA ELETTRONICA VIVA

Part I: Masters Every Voice

It was in Spain north of where I broke
a stoplight around three blocks
a veteran taxi driver yelled out his window
washers 12 stories up need no advice to you is
don't try vacuuming me while I take a nap
sun rains light   workers pick through shards
  Make every man voice rage
like a badly improvised note bodies
gotta be in tune   transport of ohm
chance this paper will fall through
tunes like clouds you expect
to hold you up break into hole and spaces
between thoughts lengthen into shadows
to dwell on daydream   someone gotta hold this
tune down on king's birthday scales his weight in gold
trombone slide down banister into Miles Davis
star dome come out outside freedom inside
freedom slavery pause and air and
  Many evangelical vultures would fall from their perches
singed by the viscera sucked through these horns blare
distant blue Fredrick smiles smiles but only empty beer cans
rehearse in their memories ending with a tune these five time
apart between waking sleeping music drops into "B-line" the
  More each vary come closer buzz slower winter steam up
pipes would freeze if they stop   what horn
got a multiple tongue to speak the
  Manifold energy vault glory some morning
when air too still to stir gauzy curtains
eyes stuck shut can breast the tape
(how triad of me)
  Makes every vain gesture speak low or sweeter than
you'd dare expect me   splattered with mud shattered by sun
could appear

More even virtuous to someone who thought art work
More even valuable bittersweet gesture   able
to say I'll pay the check or
More even view myself squeakier
Maybe even victim and demand redress like workers for
500 year bondage or women 5000 year octave attached
to shoulders shakes under blind lights   down to a croon
smoking drinking not bother thinking tomorrow

Part II: United Patchwork (Programmatic):
Breakfast in Berlin with Lots of Coffee

Waltz   what thighs beneath a dress doing
waltz and rush of patchwork fabric mind
waltz dangerous   no return   chandeliers and Linzer
always becoming something else   nobody needs to stop
Moreover eclectic values improvised can
Make each value
Meld entirely virtually everybody can hear
broken up funny void running through blackout
and wake up in a gas station on route 40 in Kansas
City woman tobacco stain yellow on her
barracks of parents about to be sued for
we are a unison strapped to a critic's bedpan no way out
but through ventilators and race through
Metropolis   enough verve to return to agricultural communities
worship female deities like in the 1950's
Many even voices coincide and react only
Mixing echoes vanquish sense this is going too
fast   semi-conductors can't control this
tongue anymore   horses
flying off merry-go-round   help
there is no solution but love   bull
there is no solution but love   hang on
there is no solo these five
ache between cool sheets
every limb in a cast floating down yellow river in bamboo unison
Means every voice together

Melody either vice or sentiment such as I could never be you Chinese plum blue which
Means electric foot-binding narrative
of dynasties histories chastities no wall long withstand Yangtze or young minor
second met my lord you rice paper boat how short silkworm
Misery can't be rolled up like a mat
Eulogy for musicians each voice
Victory heterophony
so no one suspects we bring
you yourself you cast out you in a note
always becoming something else

WILD PALMS

He floats through the air
is composed of nitrogen, oxygen and trace
a finger along her ease
the daring will feed the eye with longing
to be bored and fulfilled by a human
being none other than he who
on the flying trapeze moves gracefully

Timing is the key she pleases
my eye but trouble to bend a kiss
your dear sirs that is friends
who have my sympathy but do not understand
ideas are invaluable and value free
reached into his breast
pocket and pulled out the bean which six
times before he'd shown his readers his son runs
up yelling dad dad don't it'll spoil your dinner
to get down to business in the United States
is tied to charity whereas it used to be chastity—
lock the door, my love he has taken away

Once I was happy like an old coat
numerous a connecting pipe
but now I've said no to her manifold
and essential but few laws she never said
lock the door….

He floats through the air
and leaves no trace but hair cream
open to adversity in the jet stream
of his arc drawn from innocence rather
drawn to it by the ears flying associations
at first disapproved of Dumbo, levitation,
Icarus (here conspiracy is whispered
on expensive ships) if you make a right

turn in the labyrinth the next must be left
they say it must be forceful
difficult to be beautiful movement
graceful grateful verses plow
the rich chernozem so in love
she'd not leave off kissing him
while he talked buffeting
the air with her smacks

In Case

1981

In Case

3.
Crushing idiosyncrasies. Puffed up with abstract expressionism, her three-year-old voice made my skin crawl. A rabbit war : you think it's for smoked salmon? Soda—Lunch. Leon Spinx got great teeth. Exile by transformation. Domestic fortitude. Refocus this to read yourself. What we're doing, colors how new inflects plus. They are sisters : We are brothers. Tip toe to mean. I used to be black, but now I'm condescending to my material.
&
Trying to say appears in flood as let down your hair along the vice. Done dead, then you have me. Mandibles noise it about that anonymous knew for sure how sore they'd be until confronting the savagery of their attacks. We left him at food. More weather it out. Left there waiting for the season in which rain's rain when it rains. Head still on the body, but not as its owner would have liked. The colonel of pocket parks among practically all available precipitation day and night furrowed in files as the day comes misspelling assuredly assuredly. Indoors and out there like a scarecrow lapse. One out of a hundred strikes something in Maine. We know what she'd think, so steeped in rational cans, but possibility drives us on as year after year he placed flowers on her grave, Hartford, defamatory, belated name of nobody; her smile from the bath worth a whole day like that… Then she went on in the next county, some country, on our way to gosh, always in a slow to do, when pines and bush prickle up against the moon. When some Tuesday as dust off the road swept through the barbed wire, dust from the other field. He had his head on light, field of vision obscured by blood in the corners of his eyes that Bran would not notice from good fellowship. It was blue, grey, green, brown, all the personal colors in nature that supposed so much of our time was inhibited by attempts to speak, tongue swelled in such people.
&
The Hudson lies: building (a). Banks alternate articles and, foreshortened by carp, proud as Tigris masgouf bobbing on the map's waves, nervously look over a fin, rush drops up to Albany semi-daily along starch and gum additives. The imperceptibly touching wall, Peter remarks, holds a heart of murder in his hand, a nuts and bolts saga of future self-aggrandizement. I'd like to tell you how it is, but I don't know any more from Tokyo midget auto models as delivery systems for poisons or bio-rhythms as manipulated suicide, means softer that military. We got over who dies, who sexes, who pines, who walks the spine of the Rockies

overlooking sunset and sends no postcards.
&
To let you go means unclenching my fingers. To go means move knees forward. Why? Where? Five p.m. Sunday. Your husband takes a trip every two weeks? Imaginary breasts...baby smell...rubber nipples fill egg cartons, ambition martinified. We'd lick those A-rabs in a minute. Unspoken theory, like persons we imagine we'd like to be in love with. Almost easy offer except my books pack ink in every line dear, but I never say even to alleviate that.
&
Two capitulations: Plethora jellies, where the Persian Gulf would empty into proof. Doing it is proof. That it is alongside all of us doing it for want of it. I mean aren't you tired of, climbing ladders to a sill or underline clenched by the sandy edge of the stream? Ron or Peter or Peter and Ron bicker because they wear the same shoe size. Program artillery by millennial desperation, they was being chased by the sea until we splash up on the beach in a Lucite sphere. (Every sunbather says what (their skin is quite pink)) and we remark what brought us to this point. And here we are being rejected again at the door where only a warrant or gunpoint will go the limit near my hand below the bed in extremis about to white out the future with a phone call. Let me hear a bell ring and I'll know what to say to you. I know what to say. Say it damn it. Why did you say it?
&
The general feeling of effective in a program hardly does justice to going on, about and under my business in this case, follow-up reports, wound charts and autopsy reports being guidelines to procedure. Anyone, however, could say the same thing. I woke feeling terrible and felt terrible all day. I could hardly. A sedan comes around blasting and I drop to the sidewalk behind a hydrant, squinting to get the plate no., missing, because my eyes fill with tears from knocking the wind out of me on the unscrewed fire plug cap broken off its chain in an effort keep cool. My shoes feel gritting and shower under the trickle while bullets rule the atmosphere. Rather than feeling refreshed and alert, I touch and alienate D.A.'s witnesses, getting nowhere by referring to my feelings and making me out of them, since you don't understand that they mean you. Paragraph, masculinity. The jovial mood of the crowd supports an orange drink stand velvet rope I stand behind as you pass in your perfume. I remembered it just before they hit me with a blunt, bygone spirit of the 60's. Technical problem's been solved in the studio and we continue to be alive.
&
Menopause itself should not discredit a woman, but no one considers supporting

it. Can I call you back in…three minutes? More waiting pays custom about comfortable. This is no time to get finicky. Nothing anyway baroque around. Your bureaucrat's skepticism: I let my say slide through her, then examined the way out to view remains. We heard this over and over and were waiting for the vestiges to bronze. She told him what she had told us. After we were through, it was late as late could be, and twice I interrupted to say something, but reinforced my silence finally each time a gulp. Jealous visit very elaborate. But finally, what he meant came out. Finally, it belongs ahead, to participate in lusty give him a bad time. It's not enough to be just human you gotta, what's more, not a word could I, regardless really what we'd seen and knew was the case, clearly a matter of misspelling held over him five years and what was that compared to how I feel about human dignity.

&

He knew she knew he knew him knew her knew he knew him. Every fire custom, lady, don't throw yourself about the truck. My own infraction means nothing to me if I don't feel bad, honest. Why, Ralph, I never knew you cared. Who I know. He posed her pose for her. They had farted around long enough, but habits linger attentively. Just to clear your head about that saying something business, there's no way it's constructed by fluid overdrive, sought and feared with wild-eyed resistance.

&

Meanwhile other bodies, wings darned by ears, would sooner call nothing without shape, but it occurs at moments, by bread alone, the time I began to mix, giving way myself to be returned from the door she sent me to, across deserted areas, figure already my hand could not touch. Desire to do it gets me going, then thinking of, difficulty that could be encountered by attitude.

&

Let me go, let me be, let me stay, I'll do whatever you say. Here, you like these I don't, student loans, evidence, besides I like rugs on walls. Or bones the last man found in his fish. No way to be only. Less capitalization than possible. End the business, reroute feelings and get impotent. Ha, she said then. Just careful. How usual crowd extremities leaked away into another epoch attitude. Airmen jotted down through cumulus to accumulate data again. The future a thinner present. The airmen jot, mermaid. A deliberately manhood type let her go her way. She's not interested; she's no trouble. Get out so much taste, but no one's willing to take one. Anti-aphorism addict. The little clicks make music to mean. July 10. Hear it. Starting tune conducted:

&

Later tiles, an add craven with Sunday's, we bs*te the the, (I like Listless. We opt out, pick over an alluvial selection, the better to hug with restless plunge. How do I owe a metaphor allowance? Bob envelopes before such. Later Loonies : A broken chicken. Marxist glosses, 45 rpm hem and...chartreuse. I know her, but she don't know me. Always had strong feeling, smell ambition, muscles, farther from, ersatz, older. Those novels and what slats pose as people detergent the. I always wait to see those large colors. ERE 3) so you're one, too. What baseball that (o yes we do…Attribute)). Do it go the far. Almonds 1) raw 2) cooked 3) sugared.
&
We have a lot of close animals. The one left really was me. I'll like to so… Whatever you say, only say I could not say. Stitched by the bar and allowing firth, or a name at a distance like triangles tension fretter rain by the flush polite. North? Yes. Shouting ex new clothes, —I got a green one and a purple one.—. (Going on morning star vanity.) Breaking in with words, the customer is entitled to recompense of self; some anyway cannot be denied, but by surgery they have in other cities here legislated against superior pressure. To find out the crazy outside feels sorry, too. The murdered man don't feel nothing, so don't get any fancy ideas about writing in your head. I'm protecting property, period. (Sex possessed generations mingle. (You always think so where you're alone.)) What I forget, my weakness, for flies, stroking, divining, Indonesian light-blasted monkey.
&
When I speak, I make money, it says; doesn't ever shut up. Don't use it to confuse, please. I'll sit and think as long as you want, then I'm. What was wrong with him let him finally see the important clue, which. He sweated in the car; he rubbed in the subway; he became Orion; he fled no further, but stalked the receipt please to sell sleep.
&
Why didn't he ask? How to know whether it was pride or that he simply didn't want to? There is something else? There isn't anything else? What is claustrophobia? How many eggs chicken? He left? He gave a chance? He vomited and vomited? There is no pattern to moon? Faded lines, the stars follow rein? We are getting very old? Collect adipose? "Overgrown conscience?" Matter of fact unreason?
&
The changed point of view relieved me so I almost cried taking the part of that near frantic man whose friend he had divined was dead. You accidently stumbled through the screen into the read once again where connections they were. But I

was not carried off but dropped it in this cup for you to find. His acumen did not lessen one. A mirage, an institutional tongue : Basics to back with others.
&
Although the end the detective only solves (materialize from the 25th century with the genetic clue from the letter the murderer writes before his birdseed suicide fails). Not even science can bring back the unknown for long, overlapping papery summer. The lizard plays along this faith that if you read it you get excitement questioned by conscience, more writing than literature. And we'd let them down the knot of another vivid hustle, the huntsman still at large in the grey and green town, on this large and ancient river that bleeds her. Here we cried taking the part of that near frantic man whose friend he had divined was dead. The you accidently stumbled through the screen into the read once again where the connections were. But I was not carried off but dropped it in this cup for you to find. Unusually, his acumen did not lessen one. A mirage, an institutional tongue : Basics to back with others.
&
Why let customs doubt? Red planes and white corridors, blue and white future Mediterranean or L.A. under sail. Plus la. Is real fun the suppressed excitement of the heart, intellect qua? Is real fun 1848? Dear me, What have we here where I feel for you in the dark? Hand lens comes in handy right at the end for nick in heel trod, trace traced. Time returns on a raw planet… Are you still reading? Fill in the attractive but masochistic young woman with a secret, the politically ambitious businessman who's transparent, the society portraitist, the spinster, the kid, the mother, the son, the stolid police sergeant, the dog lover, the mad scientist, the inefficient bureaucrat paranoic, the postman, the in any case.
&
On the off ramp that her lead might volunteer some mention, I took the drive to Southold. Cruising the L.I.E. my mind returned to the same question, —Should I drive so fast, after all the oil crisis, is that a speed trap, don't push this guy he's crazy, why don't I have air conditioning? It was a mystery. The only thing was. Untouristy enough. This has got to be the. At last a roadside inn and bar run by three retired impersonators. I sat down and ordered a beer. All the way back to the city I pondered the question, —Should I signal, is this lane faster, will I get there by, should I use the exact change lane, was that Patchogue?—
&
In any case the subject filled (I out explain myself (heretofore, cool cryptic),) let me go now, details awry, if you'd only remember, does her letter mean… Postmark, a sweep of the hand, bundled them into the car at the time of the

arrest, pushing down on the heads. Posh jail. Final solution : punch maw. Let him slum himself. Elements of fire. Surrogate pesterer. We get back to where I was drinking coffee in front of the radio. Discover first. Wet sentence each major clue. Wrung later. Your dollar. Waggled his head. —Well— she said… Herman and Dahlia hung on the bar as I entered the Madonna Club. He put down telephone. Muscles relaxed around her mouth and her eyes opened a little wider, causing mascara to flake, in her own image. The word "oh" popped out like a pin had penetrated her gluteal epidermis. —The last I seen her.— And Lieutenant Press, and Sergeant Dude, and the ballerina all left for Lake Winnipesaukee. (This should please the French.) She looked at me again and again. So uncomfortable he had an air of ease. (You don't understand a word? Well, then, look at it that way.) Brute was puzzled by the Flako's tone, but nobody else blinked; it was all out front. That's hard to say right now. A small man plush in the front, dome top, all the air of straight surgery. All right he killed her and she killed him and he killed her and then there was a gang-style execution and that about wraps it up for all except who wants still to know what for. And to them I gives the...

&

In any case the word you use a lot in this business takes on a new slant when applied. —You ain't got no style.— Try proof. By now I can smile. Meanwhile another worry lump sum, quanta. It was the kid, lethal pigtails and jovial. I bent over double, irregardless the lease. There is no end to understanding, intended to skip. Yes, in a way. How can they think enough will? There for some service. Allow me out, irrespective odds, your histories and biographies, dream angel, it's enough that. How please so can try? Let it seep in a whole night coffee. Jealous motive moves his visit. (I told everyone I'd be one so now I'm being one.) Relinquish hold now and lean back so the acrid smoke. Your lettuce. You letter. I present money, kisses, water, leaning in occur for you. Two floors above hers. Let yourself down from expect, easily on your daybed. Read the whole estate and you know who had a motive. Not to satisfy but to say, but… Sleuthing the period for suffice.

&

In any case I rummaged and tried the Murderer's Times, some except anybody's life. She stood tall, but felt short, just you and me will go on being us. That maybe. But comes through rebus. (And then they look and like a word, so give em.) Staring at nothing, where nothing edge, blank fad, really characterless diamond cut, and a princess of absence : Wind blows meaningfully, now it moves forward, tracing toast smells… As a doctor and his wound tended, we wrapped it up. Drinking us in toward a declaration of space, a space we move, a space we bunch, a space wherein, a pretense for. San Francisco. I watch the face accrete from his scratching… I made $1800 in fees and overcharged $435 worth of expenses. All in all I felt satisfied with two months' work. The pressure, the articles aligned, the creeps ensconced, the letters aligned, the feeble dead, the rich aligned, the merchants relieved of some of the case, the self aligned, the priest lost all his wares to me, the suffering aligned.

&

In any case what wasn't there? Oh you know I still love you very much, it's just that, it must be my digestion, weather isn't my, I'd hoped we'd see each other again real soon. I'd made my play and you'd made fun, at different times, sometimes the timing is off. Each wait until they had every little detail fixed in? Never. The suspect's done time, you too to see these upright citizens make a play at being. Yes, in a way. OK with her. Now you are satisfied. Carried to the floor her feelings. I lifted her eyelid. Don't say boggle. Any invert. The phone rang. The answering service to find out if I was leaving. Then what he told you this morning: We killed off a certain number. Next time we'll get more. Simply in preparation? He told her there was no question. He was wrong, make it question. She looked up at me and drooled a little before she spoke.

&

In any case decors shape and sate. Keep it aspiring. West left field. Where the blue cup grips, pretty and honest, well sure, fine, but then how often would we edge closer. Always smiling to make sense or pressure, pleasure, sump, braille, yes it is just… look at the words of his letter and it's obvious that he meant, did not mean. He left her no choice. He attempted her and she was tempted. We left field and skirted the redoubt, finding along. Stumbled on a few and now centered in the ring of black and white flashing bubble gum machines, blanket thrown over the whole obscenity to examine the nap. No science really, no points like that, a look around like we expected to find us all eating granola a lovely morning, sunny, dewy, birds and the like pointing and pointing and now it's like this.

&

In any case gets regular toward the end. Maybe someone did it. Maybe they had reasons. Maybe they solve it. Maybe there's no story otherwise. So what? Not for the story, not for you, not for me, an effort pulling back covers to reveal the skinned remains.

&

In any case he killed himself and they killed each other, so no one really was left but me with a bad taste, too easy to sell, too east, too. But most of the people are out of their minds. Even the Texaco tanker captain frisking off the Grand Banks and the mother of four in Colorado must.

&
In any case spare them, deride their expectations as much as yours, perspicacious reader, who for a few minutes at least, while sitting out on the stoop playing with your toes in the August night said an ambulance rushed by. A turtle of two schools. I don't know if I prefer the one proclaims the rich walled or fools think so. No more waiting. Let's get things out in the open.
&
In any case, she hired to assuage; she could have paid more. They all divorced. The pacemakers kept us on time and her periods endeavored to. It ended an era and recognized another had already commenced; weather and gun left a blank, hardly enough, a stop on the right, yeah, sure feints, why not you, me, her, let's all, why not a stiff one? But always in the back. What can I expect? Her still trim figure slouched off to the solarium. I turned up the air conditioner and spun the dial to .99.
&
In any case if inflect over you, remain what you always were—a beautiful face. I know you tried hard to pass, but that's no reason for tears. She planted all the clues I could think up. They outfoxed each other 27 times while I waited twiddling my thumbs. What more can a mustache do? Your nose over an ice cream soda held that length about three months. Inflation by greed the most time, unexpurgated at worst. But a "speak", she's no less than, with a shadow pain, paid, sound incision, cracking knuckles in the space, aging in the space of no thankfully final solution. We make a go. Live out of suitcases and later an Irish bar. Corridors. Shake of unhunched, clicking life in the grass and weeds, Pearl singing near the outdoor shower.
&
In any case encased in a cloud of non-case, non-case general, compulsive by criminal, this nation of them remains my alibi. (Skidwork our specialty.) Protégé of ambivalence, he was happy to be happy, and she was sad to be sad. No matter how hard boiled remains an egg. I had too often to excuse myself during an inquiry and push past the lady of the house to her toilet or bolt. (Trivial proximities.) As garbage pulls the first commuters into their places behind composition boards, summer crimps. The grid exists. (The grid does not exist. (The peel off gives a sense of. (Let and keep track. (Presume to confer.)))) He leaned over the corral fence. He jumped, he bled, he lied, he ate eggs, he sent me a phone call.

Converses

1982

ODE

package MY—Package is	. the visible and private parts
	. form the package specification
	. this is the visible part
private	.
	. this is the private part
end MY—Package;	.
package body MY—Package is	. this is the package
	. body
end MY—Package;	.

IS WOULD SHOULD

I haven't but would . move to is
    so? go GO .   ward you on
however : quickly . with sudden palms
jade . =
    must help .   a(nd) more
    all the time .   for me
        you : me
        you   me
        you :   me
        you   :   me
(pregnant with carriage) . shutter contains
    who : did .   get used to what
    and would say .   stingy lovers
    I've been .   bless of spoil
    and would .   springs
opposite hands same poles. who guides

no oughts: come:now.   trouble
red ***and*** green   .   'cause : thought of
it

potato   wheat   rice   rye   cane   cane   rye   rice
wheat   potato

MY HONEY

Now let's see . Later too late
come and get it . what circles
here I . it? us?
what? . what
wash hands first . the burgher's board bared
then offer . and backside
here to and for . the truth about
for get it . until now
(purpling) . holy
HONEY . eat of
well of all the . we eat it, and ate
noble . until we ate us
and last moment . they gone pastrami
we realize and . sweet life,
clam up . honey
honey . what

what . how misery has
been
how history shows . about it (all)
comprehensibility and unity. there is no le
left
honey . none, no one
ever increasing conquest . a last effort to
break
of material . into
and development . before it’s
who asked you . it
honey! . stoic

I REMEMBER HAVING MET HIM

Had . stray hand
    I remember . simmer
but had . tea shadow
    remember . extinguished
It began, had course . (tense
    meandered into sand . unwieldy)
as usual . grove in
    is there never . gravel
        some . .;,.:’.

LEVELLER

This . Demonstrate
is . what
'how' . it's
example . of

Methods , of determining
structure , from motion

MUSICAL GRAMMAR

Sentence, period . Vulgar boatman (person
to use)
    breathless .   leap to mind the p's
spoke on intake . to 'hold it' please
notate . Puvis wires
and descriptive . modernize
    of the meanings .   (formica)
of—
of . turn dreams to say
Sentence is. . complete
    noun verb punctua- .   musically
tion
in grammar . filtration
language notes . hear a clue
Note the uses. . long arms and small
    notice not notes .   I know'd was me
who asked you . selves conscious
    I did not ask who .   that purpose

CLACK AND TONE COIL

Now you begin to . label curve
see
who? . point, there.
no what I am getting . I'd like to b/c. funny (ca.)
like where . clown
let's clear . coin-a-phrase
the air (afraid)
her face is . lack-a-duck
white
and her . turn, crimp or fold
ankle...
who? . along read it
what turns and . by the b-b-b
mushrooms
and eek or ooo . or ck for camel
that page and con- . intertalk (prehensile)
verse

through tune to con-   a (r(e(volve)))
tinue, a shun
and turn for the worms   . rise   home   clues
up to where I (a) tell   . neither firm nor fixed
have dug in and run-on   . about the digit integer

broke   .   / = /
the   .   so & so
then corner   .   lightbulb
.   ...

AND THUS BEGUN

Be at home . maid

tv material . yes, m'apron

you are lounge . (((

and serve her cubes . –

Be at home . f.

for her sidereal . sweet.

and long to . science? Real

proper air . too I

& with it . got rhythm

you do . prefab

you will . altruism

grasp . squawk

and with it sphere . y'hear

Now wait . tiptoe through

hold on . ...

better dream . &

plumbing

FRERE JACQUES

if were to take . one old food
if were to take . to heart
    of thee I .   burn
    cling .   churl
    allusive allure of .   whilst I praise.
how context doth pretty , drivel
the tentative point. , screw
as in . and in : , mortar
and in ... , pacemaker
which you'dn't , cataract
    Pledge and range far ,   seriously plaster
from mate to uneasiness , th———
    I lie ,   cut water
I know , yes, pepsi
I lie , the person
    you liar ,   huh?

but inside out I , strive to be hoaxed?
        what ,   except
that is in is out , oh
— in O , sol
        when we used to ,   burns
got a cigarette? , match

U-HAUL

me off every verse . it yourself
because it's not on . unwilling elaborates
and then giggle . (yawns)
at every turn . let it
fuck you then . let it not
ok . concludes
in it's . hyperbolic let
helix for adversity . lest stray
you're being silly. . abet
I had a fortune . and spill out out of
cookie shape
Great Good Fortu- . of a solid
ne

UVULA

la
        la la
(dropped for sound)

                                                                                . la

WHO WAS THAT MASKED

what we need . a year ago to rescue
of ourselves . no, two years
    daddy-o . so of
gesture inward . shadow . .
calls pineal . try to mingle
to rear . an a the he
    cute . permeate
    but you're no . "gross body"
I'm " & * . trance forward
    but not . to ***un***point
        AWAAAY . colonize, critic,
removes
    you who . charity but me
    mr clay pigeon . char chore
        ma'am . comment, elixer,
selfless?
    look out . a cloud obdurate
        thanks . poemechan.

pain pain . learned to eat from Tonto
it'll soon . preserve
this or this . perservere
don't worry . in sarcasm, into
earth
such imagination. figure: remand to the
heap
and manly vigor . with our clothes on

A.K.A.

Charles Brown	.	Chuck wrench
"Charlie"	.	Metonomize
Sgt. "Ape" Brown	.	& as the oNe we call
St. to his rue	.	person as speaking to you
binary another	.	abab
ABCD	.	beautiful rationality
"far from"	.	we'll like to go
once sd.	.	distant associates
sp ce a ?	.	de la troisieme type
we have wt.	.	O grav
and conj.	.	and magnetize
yet prob....	.	you North, me Tarzan
RSVP St.	.	in place setting
RSVP & sing. we	.	the napkin cloth
to two ones	.	married
all go to C....	.	the cog

Why it's . fits the gear
Screw Loose . aloha
A.W.O.L. @ alt. . Y'all real soon now
piece . it
and f.v., i.e. . C.O.D., etc.
Over the hill except after . third party
We three achieved . who doesn't exist
naut. hist. . subject
yet at NAB j t begun . rock and toll
I leap up . some fine
and down . known like
boys boys . too
that's him ok . subject arrow
Potroast Chuck . anchors
parole fuzz . suh

LOVE SONG No. N

He want . n
She want . o
    it .   P
it it it it it . (s)he

CON PUNCT.

Could you? . †
Will she . I b
    I didn't . +
    or & . ...
oh yes . also &
    a hem . ring
    you were "ing . Oh, I say, old man
If I . /
Will he? . *
    The name is . %
where was . ! continue
    now now . sweat and sweat
wrote more then than now . † not prod.
    no end . no pause
    . = mind . yrs.

TELLER

One cage to another . Alien
        signs . Jaws
        hi . Ten
the line . Casablanca
        " . Night and Fog

CARTOON

We talked it out . start first
and now it's gone . then lable
Carnival . choice
I would be you . multicolored pig
with my problems? . coyote
and you would be me . play jurize
with problematic . coot
I would continue . to get at
yeah . oh oh
let's eat . too late

YOJ

typed	,	(cbp) ace
leg fur	,	poem on
zoid	,	the occasion
crescent	,	of having
census	,	written it
Zipperstein	,	cat's contacts
All the king's	,	keen liasons
help	,	so
long term rational sensi- bility	,	gout
Help	,	loud shebum
you call?	,	you give?
what you want	,	fete
I?	,	loose
Want?	,	spin in
But...	,	content (w/) (is)
I? Want?	,	contraries

Well, well, weld , span
Certainly , and descending
spiral
And of course , both read both
then
A word beginning -)
with the letter
What letter? , bloodlet
What you want , p’tit
whenever , so
just call I’ll bet , mood
NOW ME HERE , (chorus)
allow me to consult , (alternate chorus)
moonad , lipid
noiq , sever
heh , quick

IDOL

cense with a thurible . no invention
    allocates all the fun to   sentimental & bitter
himself
    (so jovial) .   debaucher
genuflect . (Sadistic in knickers)
    allocates all the fun to   word = therefore
himself
    (so sad) .   the world too us
allocate to the nursery . (give up, bud)
    would have had had .   statutory
we not
    (mock Blake) .   talk
a bed clothes rope . Makes me mad

NOW NIGHT AND STEW

What a homely scene . Were you nipples
what do you want to . periods, I would
run-on
why not tell how. but where
beyond light . these, them geist
patter . heil dem
the place . dat/tonight us unite
where you who . only in this corner wea-
ring
wood feed . flies she is on
FLAMES . and costs rise

ORDER

each . line obliges
clears . you slip showing
for . ever = alike
next . ... super
  together . what relations ant.
  being . is so
  too . echo
  horny . ten hup 2 3 4
the sexes must be . degrees given in hot
educated separately. each
then turned loose . annotated so we know they
want
  to . literature first
  have ideas . then.

Popular Fiction

1981-1985

EPISTLE APOLOGY

Riding from the capital to my home in New York, I noticed that autumn was still intense here in the south and I thought to write a poem, a posteriori, that would, by its rhythms transmit the rush and transition of the season, but full of regrets for not having been able on my trip to formulate or remember answers to certain questions that had been put to me about myself and my work, I am attacked by anxiety that the placid beauty of leaves changing color out the window of the train cannot alleviate. All the pieces are present; I have merely to put them together with procedures that...or are the procedures laid out yet.

Autumn is when leaves get very colorful as they are dying, a high culture phenomenon. The remnants and abilities—profundity, rationality, spontaneity—have a great impact on the senses, but because what will happen soon is so obvious that it's not really threatening, except through fear of change, most remain increasingly calm throughout. And it's not a mistake either to go about our business or to shape what was too unformed to emerge this season into a thought that can be stated next spring when we have another chance to reach more people.

With certain friends I feel compelled to know more about myself and to express it more clearly than I would or even feel is true. The brilliant propositions distilled from years of labor that seem to abound in the great literary, scientific and philosophical works of the past, but are more simply perceptions of particulars, are too far away to be grasped completely in every conversation and in any case can only come out from an explanation of how I feel in all my inconsistencies about a given topic and this itself, which I often don't want to admit, incites my mind to riot away from forthrightness which is its refuge.

These breath of autumn thoughts, mutated into strange shapes by generations or a nodding acquaintance with someone somewhat beyond critical mass, do not have the clarity and impact of the leaves peaking, and I feel more comfortable, that it is scaled, as I ride to where the leaves are all on the ground and the branches up in the air. It is less exciting, but to speak nature as well as the honed abstractions of native discourse is to remember all the dialects.

On the other hand I can only convince by being myself. The rough edges showing in the thought in the rhetoric is a way out of the abysses of mind and aids insofar as communication is possible. The notion is elitist, but I don't think that the elites will support it either just yet. This is because a multiplicity of languages, as distinct from a universal language, which by now can be seen as praxis, includes science and technology languages, genre languages written in detective novels and science fiction, Black English, even literary language, that is, all one thinks to say in the way one thinks it, and as such is a recursive concept the ruling class cannot sustain.

To accept that complexity does not have to be unified or that unification is packaging language for consumption is to understand both the plan and the intention. To skirt an issue to give it credibility and leave a hole where itself is and assume that will be seen as intended is an aesthetic that can only survive in its nest, impossible outside of art, although I am here pointing to where this started.

ABOUT

This is about about, until now a subject reference, point of interest or city all roads converged upon. This is about about; to say what it's about and to be about it on all sides, around its house, in circuit, around the outside, here and there, approximately, almost, also includes a reversed position, in rotation, colloquially, near, in the vicinity, all round, in the neighborhood, not far from, on the verge of as a gerund (about being), concerning, but no longer "the subject" or what it's "about", more in the original sense of outside. It is the indexed subject, a space of nouns, persons in action, the words that pertain to their vicinity and intention or set them off by opposition. Space is made for a subject by delineating around it. The subject is what's left over: Not the thing, but what's about it.

Such non-referential and abstract modes express characteristics; for example, beauty is about ends, the spaces between our points of view, that is, about the corruption that fosters it—a possibility not out of line with traditional notions of transience, which is presented as an alternative to narrative creation, clothes that do not fit or are artified to appear to fit. The emperor's new clothes concealed nothing, and one can see now he is naked.

NOTHING

That of which many large varieties are found in the major cultural centers of the United States. Although the eminent Earl of Rochester, John Wilmot, has somehow ascertained that Nothing was the elder sibling of Shade and spoke to it as to a familiar, the modern variety seems unrelated to anything in particular, itself derived from nothing and going in that direction from which it came.

Nothing, as implied above, is derived from nothing, although translators of Hindu and Buddhist literature have more often found nothing to be a prefix of Ness, unrelated to the Scottish monster, which is only nothing coincidently. In colloquial terms nothing is what one has "plenty of", and it would not behoove any compilation of contemporary learning and culture to omit.

Nothing has been called dust, void, eternity, but materially shirks these aliases in modern times by being considered merely metaphysical, preferring the contemporary tendency to ascribe importance to the particular and objective. Its opposite seems no longer something since these days the opposite of matter is anti-matter, not doesn't matter; hence the modern tendency to construct nothing as a noun or person, making light of it by "little" or much of it by "big", the latter of which in this increasingly hectic age has tended to thrive more than the former.

DISINTERMENT

Producify by exclusioness
give by subvert
replumb or dismake shiftment
submonition to Thursday

Dismorphology   Unheraldrate
Rememberment   deassurify

Ok to refriend (stamp)
depertinent takeability
unmongst
rephrasatory unfemalization

Disregard, recoriate pairitude
comparement of sculpturority: defile (side) vs.
unremergement as selfification
safed to suspiciate, not reever, simplicon of nonfinement

uncontinued deferral of reselfizationicity
cat-meow yellowize
unregenerate redigressivity
unlistening, hand descention from wrist
prechandelierizement digiticity
deconnoiter hydromarinertudinousness
foppitude respite feminotropicity
desophisticate identizoid—African sculptines

WEST INDIES EXERCISE BOOK

Apart from the Barthian deviation of genre writing, taking over the 'universal' bourgeois writing style in 19th century Europe…

Can we reconstruct our written world by a coalition genres, interlocking genres, substitutions of words from one genre's vocabulary into the kinds of sentence structures of another, stereo thinking in one genre on two thoughts, stereo writing in several genres on one thought, extension of normative grammar as a genre, e.g., using sentence structure as a genre, extending the possible 'correct' sentence structures to include several sentences linked by commas or two thoughts linked as if they were one by normative grammar, or 'correct' sentences that do not really become a full thought until they have grown into a paragraph. Or instead using the paragraph as the repository for a single thought, determined by metrics or tones of vowels or becoming 'clear' only after several such sentences have been compounded.

What genres can go together? How many are necessary to make an inclusive global language?

What is synergy here?

Can we imply global language by imbuing the genre with the details of doubt that imply a systematic process behind the apparently limited genre or is that analytic and academic—the alternative being additive and synthetic—grammar and content?
How can we show the relationship of extended grammars and layered genres except by making meanings specific? (This writing as philosophical genre of meditation (but fiction 'cause of my elliptical mentality.))

Can uncertainty become a mechanical and neurotic process? Only reasoning within the discipline (as Wittgenstein says yellow-green with respect to yellow & green and blue-green and yellower-green, etc; as Greenberg says "self-critical tendency") can supply the assurances needed to believe what one says although some will be swayed by delivery, flash value, occasional revelation as opposed to continuous revelation of closely festooned trains of thought. But these too are suspect as derivative or constricted as opposed to journalistic revelation of fact

(supposed fact) after fact to create a simulacrum of reality—style, transparency through which the world of politics or sex can be seen as it 'really' is.
Genre writing as all other 'modern' art contains a substrate of satire. If we apply high-art taste, e.g., not too many adjectives, not too much sensationalism in action or language, then we satirize our own intentions because we apply such seriousness to Flash Gordon or Lew Archer. If we apply standards of genre taste, e.g. 'let the good times roll', we satirize our own desire to 'get down', sensationalize. Only multiplicity can be 'radical' enough to subdue the 'fact' that we know too much (late-city man, ennui, etc.) and send us tumbling into a state where we realize we have to be prepared to learn something totally new. But the problems of multiplicity emerge.
There is no way to objectify the relations between sensations or styles because there is no between. Between objects and styles there are other objects and styles. Between them others down to mote objects and so to massless bodies. Objects of attention (affection) describable as plasmas of varying densities. Mix societies but focus attention where we will—not taste again—and that becomes the object and then objects and so the modernist attempt to focus on the objective between sensations, e.g., existence, transition. Paradox of this kind of thinking if done in minimal terms.

But as our presence is combinative....

So Mondrian talks about relations between sensations. What are they? This is met as a proposal. In terms of perceptions, it is ambiguous, but in terms of art, it is descriptive because art has clearly divisible parts that artists use to set up relationships in their works. How can one associate them? Is that fetishistic?

(Color is additive, writings are additive: Gestalt sensations arise when the parts are tightly bound. Some configurations are dominated by wholeness. Others tend to separate into parts. The process of composition in genre is to combine the parts in such a way that they both create a family and fall into parts, parts that relate to their original nature and parts that are combinative.)

Working with the Gestalt, not of regular forms, but of irregular, complex, ungraspable forms. How can this Gestalt be shaped? Worked? Worded? Extend the faculties for recognizing such shapes—sculptural writing.

MAKING UP THINGS TO DO FOR NO ONE

To guile her illusion.
To generosity chagrin.
To similar stretches in our vices voices.
To wrap ilk-rapt creatures.
To advantage recreation.
To hire all the rage.
To finalize ideal as ... a reason.
To go on about immorality of connection. (Mixed signals make me affable for a while.)
To give the air a try.
To fly the milk.
To unlucky at both. To get to be what comes along.
To give up because it was all odds. (Live food.)

INTEGERS

1. Integers at Bay

Filch words. Wet like. Truss intelligence. Lawless potshards. Checkered rate. Your floe. Key unruly. Lydian Dickens. Template modes. Shadow poker. Over open. Likely fief. Pairing diagnosis. Vertical pagination. Her slut. Smithian conclusive. More it. Fever board. Polyglycoat nature. Rutting time. Imperium wordium. Slavery pause. That ~.~_. Suppresses goes? And on. Arithmetic surge. Some there. Or : ram. Oak spif. Pier pair. Oafline. Women liberate. Met set. Include one. Pants paunch. Pilot piduciary. Piute if. You just. Build death. Push opaque.

Garotte mystic velour. Lucky wire environs. Ignorant rectitude succumbs. I'll wormwood migratory. Hack prairie breaker. Ibex ward constabulary. Three word Walpurgis. Nice too is. Creeks plush Ohio. Family gear pan. Thresh trap repeat. So says drape. Peer all dust. We snuff parameters.

E're water it moves. Breathe pride and others. I jumped the train. Stage planks the bone. Blue water over fade. Breathe out over blue. We move its jump. Space over blue the. Pleasure in mutual next. Attractive blue out space. Which breathe it moves. The water of sand. Over move pride breathes. Which cloud wave sand. Seascape punctuation e're I. Train to the breach. Aloes skin shades refreshment. E're shift off cracks. Knit tires the sun. Space out over blue. Blue's crack is horizon. Description surface ripples Orientalia. What have I missed.

Please remember to keep clean. Safety valve with family support. A tinny subterfuge to avoid. Nelson, Richard, John, Paul, Ringo. We may find our soon. Come along, come along, Allen. Very kaolin to tell you. Blue army gall bladder fragments. The space of a pair. Pinch pink lying pink pinch. Nobody has time from to. Hypo, hypo, hypo, hypo, etc. Each last word mitigates mitigates. No jobs this week, weed. Alpaca mound presumes she'll let. Syntaxes, mellophone, allomorph conscientiously applied. Wee tooth in many dentistries. Hers senses ofs responsibilities errs. Modify grease, solvents, horizontal emblematic. Sir Gawain in green tights. America can't get enough of... You say you said it. The very Morse of it. Mortified trenchermen soupline the Indies. North reaches of the ankle. Allot fragments; ashamed he's scooped. Mach lorry can Mexico this. Meaning is transmitted through structure. Homer writers in such as.

Lacquer cosine delete intension equals. Label octagonal stop natural sponge. Each card indispensable five stud. I like rain and sex. Steno rye on a slip. The oui can demand full. Having come this far step. Agile bucket conjures don envoy. Throttle adjacent k-ration degenerate op. By me that I took. Withal the easy it ranges. Along the fine blade attic. Suburban daguerreotypes isolate childhood embarrassment. One black, one brown shoe. Consulting paper then addresses now. Long has he walked upright. Laverne appears in a dream. So you will like it. First plural drumming underneath soundtrack. Morn etch cow hamper tile. Allah poulet tint eighth contraption. Fuck u en rd ths. Plantain subway redoubt beside jealousy. To me in hoard lovers. Redolent up to the nose. Why am I doing this? Figure eights haggle each fetish. Mutually higgle, fives also tailgate. She balloons rug dust, Herbie. She corrects bleach and characterized. She unlaminated our good tub. Sandwiches rule broad finger counts. Include shadows - synonym: suggestive ornament. Translate with our resorting as foreigners. Reubens will dispel small thoughts. Used words to gratify ego. Lose track more than five. Know how to find them. Among outer reaches of snapshots. This time to go now. Many definitions rain in conversation. I want to mean you. Leather gloves killed the effect. Sex used in literature to. Actual feeling of Bermuda Triangle.

II. Durations

1. Checkered rate, rut phase, slavery pause
   checkered game: help phase, regularly pause
   supernatural game: help suppresses regularly claustrophobic

2. Lucky wire. Hack family, press length
   Peer wire hack plush three length
   peer too inconstant plush three trap
   push pour. tour serge. Ohio pressure
   push lush. Tour four. Ohio pliers.
   Crate lush. Alternate Four. Congruity pliers.

3. Anticipate succumbs. Ignorant drape. Construct demise.
   Anticipate push. Welling drape. Construct liberate.
   Constables push. Welling pull. Women liberate.

4. Humid way. Groat pride. Motorized fits.
   Oaf war. Enclosed pride. Motorized dust.

Oaf hoof. Enclosed suction. Involved dust.
Person anchor. Ooze grace. Express feelings.
Person silo. Smooth grace. Touch feelings.
Paunch silo. Smooth derelict. Touch especially.

5. like lady quarters repeat summoned formal like gear

6. the / of / and / to / a / in / that / is / I / it / for / as /
with / was / his / he / be / not / by / but / have / you /
which / are / on / or / her / had / at / from / this / my /
they / all / their / an / she / has / were /
me / been / him / one / so / if / will / there / who / no /
we / when / what / your / more / would / them / some / than /
may / upon / its / out / into / our / these / man / up / do /
like / shall / great / now / such / should / lather / only /any /
then / about / those / can / made / well / old / must /
us / said / time / even / new / could / very / much / own /
most / might / first / after / yet / two / / two / yet / after /
first / might / most / own / much / very / could / new / even /
time / said / us / must / old / well / mad / can / those /
about / then / any / only / other / should / such / now / great /
shall / like / do / up / man / these / our / into / out /
its / upon / may / than / some / them / would / more / your /
what / when / we / no / who / there / will / if / so /
one / him / been / me / were / has / she / an / their / all /
they / my / this / from / at / had / her / or / on / are / which /
you / have / have / but / by / not / be / he / his / was I with /
as / for / it / I / is / that / in / a / to / and / of /
the

7. Non-smokers permit less pushby throughout rice
velour permit less crush throughout perpetuates
velour skin charade crush heel perpetuates

8. Why leg work works deliberate

9. The foot is parse of bodies
Profess foot drunken parse family bodies

Profess steps drunken steps family steps
Gorgeous preserved return returns continuous duration
Gorgeous substitute flyback returns continuous go
Include substitute flyback associates and go

10. Disco teethe as armed display us
Disco Mohammed as pumpkin indistinct us
Herd Mohammed nice pumpkin indistinct if

Gratis bumper deft clue Mother code
easy bumper deft oleo mother council
easy vow sumptuous oleo slippery council

11. of / who / is / one / so / that

12. What might droop suffix ok angst
we might honor suffix ok duck
we plastic honor air dry duck

Plural tryt(st) hold damage close brick
plural soup ear damage relative brick
molecular soup ear out relative stairs

13. to step the get get gets

14. Narrative lit Blush contact sully machine
Blank lit January contact joint machine
Blank line January sump joint active

Lettuce crossing. Jalopy gambol. Symbiosis intimidates.
Refinery crossing. Casaba gambol. Symbiosis consequence
Refinery imbue Casaba except defile consequence

15. Sound track sump her remain coast
need track sump cohere remain poultice
Need fuel. Assignation cohere. Town poultice.

Communion ribs. Esoteric cross. Subterfuge conglomerate.
catching ribs. esoteric that. move conglomerate.
catching effect of that move to

16. closure scenic grid opened what whatchamacallit
closure hydrocarbons exemplary opened usury whatchamacallit

awash hydrocarbons exemplary sauced usury overcast
graphic privilege launch aside amenity preservation
graphic presumptuous assume aside amenity perpetuates
stage presumptuous assume that step perpetuates

17. step slide jump fall push pull support

III. Vowelic Integers

Deco epaulettes. Shakos oval. Hoping Polo. Grow soap. Noisy spinnaker. Plead spiel. Repeat putt. Vagabond eatery. Uxorial disappearance. Promulgate liner. Limes decode. Oblate inburst. Open haze. Sweeten derange. As raptorial. Expect upbeat. Ululate the. Blue noon. Groucho pellagra. Range punitive. Past presence. Simplified rancid. As flood. Minor minus. Minos deviates. Ole bread.

Albatross vertigo. Alligator mail. How white. Decipher mutual. Outlet bandage. Connubial pugilist. We go. Let's conscript. Furlough fricassee. Fresh frequency. Modulate modulates. Counter fives. Prompt yeo He type. Older alphabet. Exigency aloft. Produce errors. Thunder appointment. Jupiter rug. Adopt intercourse. Punjab pollutant. Pike slip. Hold quick. Sepulveda Cheesemelt. Notary publish. Alight pacemaker.

Wonder clover baseball. Mew wasp arrow. Weigh patient Tuesday. Misinform float heel. Whale spaghetti chess. Fate elf fee. Loose tread capon. Clovis faction pew. Myopic train fleet. Purloined Knievel spout. Rumor poori semblance. Mulch envoy retribution. Sculptor porter flight. Heavy loop caster. Export crematorium nudge. Solution deviate catatonia. Mistral corporation puck.

Knee wrench pleats. Decent gaggle sinecure. Everything silo but. These of pledge. Such boss tone. X-ray figure yard. Meek gerund highball. Hinny warmer equal. Otiose protagonist crows. Bound croon humor. Tumult tuning tunicle. Crazy separates graze. Flay laborer dedication. I I I. Cry decibels refund. Usury coordinate encomium. Obey five clothes.

Proprietary instincts reign. You flake cocoa. Mine gosling sensibility. Case of it. Bite a magnet. So orphan novelty. Creak sterling gravy. Cast of it. Greet scuffle meander. How to load. How toast poses. How to procreate. We hear to. Juice silence ladder. Music ocher pantry. As next pants. Yolk miserly jubilation.

IV. Transforming Integers

Camera closed in graffiti. Trees disclosed their shadows. Closure there trees tether. So much pair whatsoever. Near closing shadow him. Graffiti on their clothes. Close call there treat. The shade as disclosure.

Pleasure drone sun through. Than man did so. Well in Albany keeps. Giving us to submit. Man in the sun. Upstate in the well. Drones hover and sow. Please in the keep. Drone of welling feelings. Human two given rivers. Thorough about pleasing her. And keeping to himself. The keeper main-man through. So pleasant they did. Trust upstream and down. Give up his submissions.
The only external alarm. We'll leave you here. Only you alarm through. The leaves we hear. Leave externals to me. Let's only alarm them. Table leaf only you. Know is not alarming.

However intensely sensual hero's. He never gets her. She dies, he works. The meatball hero gets. Tender or less sexy. Than a sausage heroic. Heroine got no tense. As admirable as act. She however works splits. His works tends harrowing. Sensitive tendrils get tangled. Up in the narrative.

PLUS THIRTEEN

1. Usefulness
a. Interlocking zones of varied configurations
b. Colorful tools
c. Precision of ambiguity
d. Corral with the gate open
e. Nourishment

2. Anti-entropic Forces
a. Perception of subtle differences
b. Events consistent with common experience that appear as unusual occurrences
c. Shape determining use
d. Commitment
e. Lazy arts

3. Presence
a. Details reinforcing axioms that vary with those details
b. There are more ghosts around in the daytime
c. Inclusion of self as one of the materials
d. Mental processes interlock at the right moment to say
e. Synthesis I Fusion, i.e., control

4. Accessibility
a. Xanadu
b. The door out of the church
c. Toward the politics of language
d. Her swimming pool filled
e. A woman undressing behind a bead curtain

5. Approach
a. Fullness recognized as
b. The seat belt sign lights
c. Cutting the Gordian knot
d. Errors are volitional and the portals of discovery
e. Early dawn mountain time with surface fog

6. Inertia
a. Slipstreaming
b. I was just passing on my way to
c. An unusually wet spring
d. Chick hopping about on a frying pan
e. Nothing suits me like my union suit vs. monumental cottage industry

7. Fruitfulness
a. A fable or skepticism
b. Values inhere in forms
c. Prime numbers
d. Calculus: solution to paradox
e. Holidays

8. Ways of Seeing
a. The two-hole experiment
b. Recognition of limitation
c. A fog descends or lifts
d. Cathexis
e. Rbt. Smithson also ate, slept, fucked, went to the movies, etc.

9. Motion
a. Within stillness
b. Artesian well
c. Ideas in things
d. Calligraphy
e. Perpetual motion (rebirth of Jerusalem)

10. Discontinuous Functions
a. Perceived time
b. Hierarchy of concerns that changes with each application
c. Small differences in lovers' breathing
d. Conversation with a friend
e. Refusal of something to be categorized

11. Linkages
a. Waiting until a minute passes
b. Today's bath

c. The many single paths on the trail to Mecca
d. Right hand to right hand or right hand to left hand
e. Consequences of truth

12. Remembrance
a. Daze
b. A wooden house sheltered among conifers
c. The artist's studio table
d. Walking up stairs
e. Forgetfulness

13. Additional Configurations
a. Encyclopedia
b. A 'Polaroid'
c. Both
d. Attentiveness
e. Additions

THE EDGE OF POSSESSION

I remember what he said to me, I remember what she said to me, I remember what they said, we said; listen. He opened the door to the room that was hot, taking great care that the relics of the saints, cracked and genuine… "Let's get that guy."

I bound him to release me. Will I get to see you? I owned him until they spoke to me. "Thou hast forsaken the sponsor which begot thee, and hast forgotten the executive that created thee." The beast is organization. (Sex sex sex). Entice the subject around his people.

This time he will win, but as the old Chinese proverb says—Chinese Fortune. May your business fail that you will see—profound aversion to reposing in any one view of the world, refusal to be deprived of the stimulus of enigma. (But only indirectly can the landlord pay his rent.)

Now give! How can I make them understand that I am in earnest? They keep sending these priests after me. Doing it for purposes, not to develop a relationship.

Who was her mother that made her no sandwiches, casting off adjectives to carry on? It has to be us. What do you mean give up? I have to get my own.

Rushing requires such attention. (That the channel not slip. (Agent of the moment. Choose the act. Doing it while thinking about it. (Rubbernecking.)))

It is against charity and justice to expose the hidden sin, but not to uncover where the spellbinding instrument is located. (Enticement over time—scale of genre—superimposition, of unmannerliness—crusts of decorative plastics—self-conscious alienation—the possibility that you are not your brother, the zoo keeper.) Give us the energy to be friendly and take her.

Meanwhile the bell was striking all at once. Scratch the bell. (Pebbles all over the ground that describe gravel.) We stand behind our appraisal. There were three of them and one was me.

This sickly portent caused alarm among the ecclesiastics. The senators became priests of the deified superstructure. Without the liberalism that allowed our more radical stances to flourish... Now what will we do? Passivity and disenfranchisement, exile, we the demon cast out. How will administration treat the lives of the mind? Conclude to suffer? Now will you let me?

Sometimes the show is called belie. We drifted passed the quay, aloof, a partisan. Can you come over to my house Wednesday for some soup? Let Al sit in that window and give us a talk about alluding to it.

Rage backs them off sir, pleats the air. Trepidate to shape the lips. We live hand to mouth.

Many types of cancer may respond to VM-26, because it combines so well with other anti-cancer agents, increasing their effectiveness. His uneasiness of mind was besieged by reproaches from all sides.

Mechanical double, we ought to be doing something about, but I like poetry—creature, of water, in the name of, his response, not to the thing in itself, but to his knowledge of what it was before anything happened, a French beast (Romanum). Is the government revolved?

He tries to guard the tubes of solid state, rule the towels under the door, strengthen across, assaults from the soul evaporate awash in channel four: Moral rectum. Cornbeef square. Leech the museum. We were surprised when we heard the Japanese restaurant was out of sake. Meanwhile the sludge crept toward Omaha.

***

Performed when I'm standing here, just a make-believe person cheated the truck. Since we give breaks when serious or urgent, should he need surgery, a private house will be very good for our rendezvous. She's still going to be part of your life again.

The best kind of mean, knowing this as a certain person, who wanted to be present at what's more, went to confession before going into the presence of the illegitimate child.

Or is it too late for this decorous conquest. He does not tremble or change the channel. The reason is wanting to die and also show how brave and clarify that grinning face.

These are wonderful qualities in a man and believe me you are very macho. At other times I try to interrupt and sacrifice with ridiculous and indecent sayings… if I had only known how to really live. Then remove his foot in the name of Jesus Christ and order him, "Obmustece maligne spiritus."

Just waiting to get his filthy hands on everything that was hers, disputing are you in there. Hello? There are no issues escapes from his tongue and goes to a remote part of the heart and proper into a deep sleep wherein he is shown visions of next week's programming, fantastic visions of what you think you've seen. I assure you you haven't.

Even though it looks like art there will be certain deformities which arise not from an intensity of application, but the second, different and not necessarily better, that leaves him sad and full of confusion.

At this arrival of a good show the old man, filled with fear and disturbed, told the devil to open his mouth so he could fill it with manure.

Sometimes they have no choice, leaving the body in the form of "that's not all she said" and other terrible things. "What in the world has gotten into you?" And the caring will be informed about the needs of all of us in order to receive good-byes and then communicate with musical background music.

With these and other activities advise the victim continuously. Reach into the refrigerator often and very effective. The victim will lose $22.95 and threats. He should derail heart and mind. Those depressed by arrival on the floor may hope for the same. He must be.

After the ignorant and empty threat, joy realizes that spread is giving up and that he is about to leave, because part of our diet to fight cholesterol of the power and order of greasy dirt is really impressed by having a baby.

"I'm sorry, there's a grocery story," that of his companions extinguishing a lighted candle, because some of them are in the habit of staying behind to gloat over their feelings.

Really good, that's nice. They will not be satisfied until they are informed that coffee is bad so we will drink less.

I'm going to look up and down the corridor before the nurse leaves with any luck to go directly to my fault that has been designated by continuing compromises, giving her a project that will use up her time and energy to attend to the clothes and hair of your request for a definite leave of absence. The moment, so lush, so plush, goes out spotty, because I say it can be in different ways, as experience has shown.

That's the eyeopener. I want to avoid that in the form of blazing flame, your permission to leave in the form of wind, bees or ants. Sometimes the official ok is through the ears.

And I plan to go tomorrow, leaving through the heart, stomach and other parts. And I exit from hiding in the shape of a ball. And my feelings for you go through the nostrils, as a restaurant, in drops of blood and in other ways the court will recognize. But you will not believe them.

***

Remember what happened until this point. I was trying to say it to you, the candles superimposed on them while they take off their clothes. It used to be my job to torment them, but now my happiness is truly complete. So where are you? Where in the sense of…

You'd better hang onto metal or interior as well as exterior parts. According to your wishes, 'we're here' in both ways. It molds.

This being understood, I wasn't a young girl anymore. The passion never ends. She sings at her wedding. The hit man rambles on at length. The grievance is shipped. (That's why I'm here, to extend it.) Voucher's natural color changes while it isn't here, the phone ring gray or cedar color. Who would ever believe that dirty stuff?

It has something to do with glistening flakes, pinpricks in the pit of the stomach and elsewhere. Those mentioned find out how to use the words they don't dare, gathered here today to turn to spiritual remedies, to show its form, to enter into, to suit him. It's been getting crazier and crazier, and the mattresses and pillows take pot shots at such charms and enchantments, needles, fruit, hair, wax, lead figures.

The feather image of a man with head, hands, legs and arms which left everyone amazed has to be deodorized. Now raisins are a different matter, but are applied in the same manner—gold dust, incense, myrrh, salt, olive, wax and rue—brought to rest by the sin of lust, not in order to feel pleasure, but to garnish her head among the wax fruit.

Resort to I love you, afraid to have your cavities filled in order to have no permanent injury, I swear to you. You're not God; you can't give me any kind of guarantee.

To get you or get you to go, to make use of malice for a wonderful thing, talking to you in the morning, but the opposite opinion is a little brother for continued annoyance. Consecutively you and I undo the new pact for the camera, borrowing from the usurer and that's not all who is exposed of her own accord.

Why police allow some people to be not so sure. I had to tell the truth, the havoc, I feel badly too, for the wrong reasons. I know an awful lot of lawyers wish to enter human bodies and try to obtain such a dwelling place by a knock on the door. I'm not here to exercise visitation rights, nor oppress you with platitudes, but I'm going to touch you or make you go.

Exactly what do you know, being reversed and feared through idols and oracles. He cannot reach in. He cannot take revenge against that you don't know anything. I can't see Cliff inditing fantasyland.

She told me you were privy to some semblance. I'll find out believe me I will. It may be an opportunity to save ourselves from the macho, jealous, continental type.

You know that your boyfriend did it, but you want to build a treasury of how you really feel. You deserved that punishment, front row.

I'm going to be the main attraction. Yet another cause may be the sins of the fathers, your dance. To test the faithful, fresh squeezed, have a similar affliction with ulterior motives. The parrot said, "I thought upon the days of old, and had in mind the eternal years."

***

In the secular narrative of 'you stay away now' the battle and struggle with every day present themselves. Against the spirits of wickedness in high places… for that very reason you apply for the job, recognizing that Adam and Sarah are planning with humility their weaknesses. I can't talk to you privately; I can't have an open discussion with you; come and sit down with a pure conscience. I already told you about that. We had a date, but somebody else came forward.

The unworthy instrument repairs so much damage by making us feel young looking as the afflicted neighbor that with the unique presence of his manner, in some fast company, still being friends, he attributes everything to remembering, draws a salary (motive of esteem), casts out demons, to get to you then in terms we both understand, a terrible liar, did wonders with it, in spite of everything, victims of peace.

Still I think you're right, because I am sinful. Tell him yes, in thc hospital, with weapons to prepare and patience, because some of the stubborn and vigilant leave now. Anxiety of separation as nearing closeness stiffens. How lack of confidences leaves you behind with new vigor.

See through the man, per possessionem, and the other. Richard is my husband and he's not here. Frightening shapes find out by experience, with blows, pains of the body, but don't be too long. Whatever you're calling yourself now, I want you to go. Lack of obedience, obstinacy. Let go some of that tension—biting his hands, throwing himself on the ground, in the fire, in the water—take an__________.

Shakes in the presence of trying. (We have to believe that.) Childlike conversation, suggestive movement of the head and hands, the ladder down does not imply rejection, but beginning and entrance.

Mere man takes his place. Hatred of weakness promotes a crank phone call. I really should have your opinion, our mass. Call me if I can help—blaspheming, cursing, abusing, insulting, speaking without having studied the fine points. I know who you are alright.

Arouse suspicion, conjecture, conclude. Sudden change of personality, recurrent nightmares. So quiet because we're prisoners. He tries bribery, he tries approach, he tries to merely say it. Vacate and separate.

Unaccustomed howling and voices, visions, absence of feeling, restlessness, endurance and strength, glossolalia, singing, secrets, can get in, can get out... Talking to her and her face keeps changing and I'm talking in a different voice and then we're somewhere else... Slow pace of realization.

Why? Natural illness, crummy section of town, do you think you could talk to her later? Sounds like he lost his last friend comes up roses.

For his greater glory commit him. Too much despair over losing worldly possessions, familiarity, characterizes this morning. Mother was very secretive. (Flashlight on the rug, guiding.)

Try to learn the way to enter and his method of leaving. Mistreat the body mercilessly in the form of wind, rats, cold water down his back, ants all over the body.

I didn't know I could either. But you know what I can't understand...

***

A little disorder and irreverence in regard, a picture of the house, so sane, but the stories tell another story.

Ideas are a dime. Perpetrate fraud. Scandalize the people present. Where in the world do you suppose he is hidden?

The how long are you staying in town this time condemns and prohibits it, as my darling too soon, throw me up in a tree, giving them more power than effectiveness, teaches grab her and possess her. (Idle curiosity. (I say the best. (It's for sometimes. (Money burns whole.))))

Don't hesitate to call me. Don't go to the toilet just yet. Don't walk the dog. Don't go to the bank. The sense of being useful of one's neighbor. It that matters. How we got to this wording. "I'm going to miss you too sweetheart very much. And if there's ever anything you need, you'll get in touch with me real soon."
Rebuild the sand.

I heard the phone ring twist his tongue, putting the blame on everyone else, and with the first two fingers he never permits sayings or sophistries, but shuts her up with an oath or announcement in her face. So many things all at once in the body of a person, a lot to deal with. The last thing in the world I need.

He doesn't know the meaning of the word, or, a lot of empty conversation put you in this kind of a mood. He may indicate a toe in which the demon should stay until the men handling the search on this end… (For his greater torment their names are all signs of proof—tortured serpent, rabid dog or too many people have keys as it is. (Everyone but himself. (At least someone is making a living.)))
He reached for the shiny ball.

Resist loving warmth for very long nor learn from him whom he adjures, nor favors, nor credibility, but shallow talk is a sign of close connection, a lot more important than missing dinner, flattery when it comes to something serious, where the spellbinding instrument is located in your accusations, effective immediately. Who are his greatest rivals? I have to find a way to get it to get it to go, to learn the meaning of his name, without yoke, abandoned, adversary, beast, fornication, pride, avarice, investigating the stability of lovers.

(We're going to be running into each other again from time to time. (And help us out when you're pregnant, would you… never mind.))

Whose pretense has a way with women? Her reasons for wanting to leave threatened our friendship from within and without. What the fuck. Blame him for his only begotten son.
Against the despised give an eye, or replace them by the blade. To shred him raging, quickly give ear to us…

We are all standing. This is no excuse. Now that we're alone you can tell me.

She can take an apartment anywhere she can afford it. I'm going to tell her exactly that. Their faces reveal night, acknowledge your existence.

Be gone. I can hold you.

Written while listening to the Soap Opera "Edge of Night" & reading A Manual of exorcism, very useful for priests and ministers of the church. Hispanic Society of American, 1975.

The Word I Like White Paint Considered

1986

FISHWATER

Among our shared shots,
in places in the hear,
I couldn't be more there
than when I'm not here,
and I gave him my spayed look,
like a soft but self-important
If you can't stand the heat.
Well, I said to him, If you call
now I don't want to speak to me
as her thinking about herself.
Will my prow, breaching foam,
To rise across the dollar Potomac.

THE WORD I LIKE WHITE PAINT CONSIDERED

Anonymous days transact to know
the poppies on the mauve river
by narrowing down their trenches
like soldiers inhale tenuous
at a fruit stand fingering oranges and figure,
ubiquitous from South Kora to Zaire,
they're not in thrall or starving on the farm
and therefore, haven't been truncheoned themselves,
before I come to where a special knock
lets me in your movie house,
who blackout trying on gloves
with soft words inhering in ransom notes
cut from advertisements that arrive in brown
paper covers whose bedrooms are too hot
whose halls smell and strain awareness.

NO CHANCE OPERATIONS

He had a stroke of luck
where beasts lick their paws
of your armchairs and the fortune
cookie right eye of your surprising
spectacles carries the word
like Typhoid Mary, dragging bones
through green felt enough
that rien ne va plus.
His last words, "Utah Shale and Advanced Ross,"
smile where bubbles burst.

NATURAL JOB

Is your
Washroom breeding
Bolsheviks?
— 1930s Scott Towel Advertisement

Tis the season to be pause
and refresh for the new
deciduous connectors
to the habit habitat
ape fatherly conviviality,
depositing what they really mean
by perquisite, overlapping exhale
in the season of your withdrawal.

There's a reason to be wholly
unexpected about the second,
remark that the yule log's
hotsy daily in the bastions
of their slam-the-door-in-your-face
routing, of what seemed so
plump to thrash—
a fallow of a fellow.

Death befalls all slaving graces
In their dainty calumny on the job,
Smearing shit onto their faces:
One employee benefit from the mob.
Doesn't matter how much money,
When the nabob fires you, you've been robbed.
Try to tell them work is funny,
That's when grown adults begin to sob.

Our Nuclear Heritage

1986-1990

PLAIN AND FENCING RHETORIC

People like you do make government policy, by casting your analysis in directions of your own choosing—hold it!
–Tom Clancy

Primitive housekeepers unpossessed of jacks
–George Eliot

The atomization of politics,
one citizen/one police revolving around,
reduces our nuclear heritage
to its insufferable frame.

Yet we've all had commerce with identities
that aren't confined to our kind of reality
and can't be pinpointed. Even Democritus
would concede that whether all units are equal
isn't as important as once he decides
to emphasize the unit, its relations
with other units become paramount.

Now we are engaged in a great
atomic, in this sense, war
where one's ideas are pitted against every other one's,
each the property of a unique and desperate
individual cunningly inscribing signatures
on the underbellies of conjunctions that connect them,
replete with all the rules of our life in one.
The ideas we agree with are morally correct.

And yet if we accept that building weapons,
running the arms race,
and promoting the cult of the individual
is tantamount to war, isn't abortion murder.
None of your perspective rhetoric is lunch.
Such logic produces such Red Guards

as our sensibility cannot combat,
and we are reduced to parrying
increasingly torrential forces with rationality.
"There's just a thin blue line
protecting you from those animals
out there, sister."

Such mediated hopelessness leaves
us prey to conclusions, to solutions
to stem the fretwork. Conversations
about public health transform
into frenzied diatribes against Star Wars.
Shall we abandon our values,
succumb to technology's tithe? Shall we
blame it on the Beaver because we left it to him?

"Control of populations is just part of our full service, accountable innuendo. Just because we don't tell you what to do does not mean we don't care."

I do not mean that lines should be drawn though the center of the conflict surrounding mangonism, the training of plants contrary to the natural conditions of their growth. (She was so anxious not to believe that shameful thing.) The same movement or near movement, like the freeze, or anticipation is implied, so that even the most massive solidarity effort involves precise titillation of each person's inner acceleration.

"For the future stands with one foot in the present and another raised mid stride. It is propelled by the forward momentum of the present moving the shadow of the raised foot further into unpredictable chaos. The attraction of the shadow and the foot fused by light draws the present forward, a fifth force the National Security Agency seeks to harness, but we currently focus on increasing sales in third world countries."

FREE RADICALS

> *Nothing is harder than to believe in men's consistency, nothing easier than to believe in their inconsistency. To judge them in detail and distinctly, bit by bit, would more often hit the mark."*
> –Montaigne

Let us go on then,
since we are here. The first
strike decides the affair,
for who would have courage
for a second except the machine?
(Here I have become a grammarian, I,
who once learned language only by rote.)

Waves lap the shore;
the horizontal parallels
fragment the shape
of the gull like a post mortem
painting of the bird, pecking
transparent food, reframes the screen.
Science clarifies art
and politics, helping to regulate our thought.
Rather than throw the baby out with bomb,
diaper the brat. It's
art that's dangerous.

I woke up just past 3:00 am, restless, unable to go back to sleep. I didn't feel inspired, just irritable; we'd turned the heat down; it would be chilly, and I'd forgotten to put my robe by the bed. Angrily I snuggled back beneath the covers, but it wouldn't work; I was wide awake. Slowly the first line of the warning to subway riders materialized into my head, "Es muy peligroso", neutral emotionless, clear as logos, as the printed word would be if it spoke itself.

Transfigured night.
Charting the emotional extremes of a woman
who has lost her lover. Wind bag
is a foil for solo strings.

Conventional logic of radical features.

Clad in radiation proof suit, Carpaccio wanders among the pulverized bricks of the center and outward to the charred bodies. He pushes his forefinger through a charcoal skull, rubbing the cinder against his gloved thumb. The only evidence of the magnitude of this action is a slight elevation of his heartbeat.

Mar measures.
By desire.
By the fantasy of ends.
By the recycled whirs.
The prose of solicitation makes
sense by changing a few letters,
the most destructive pose of love.
Propositions substitute for truth.
Only cannibals thrive
in the romance of their own lives.

Explicit identification of any corpse misses the point, and so the splitting of the nuclear family finally takes place under the ax of the split atom of a tasteless, odorless, lighter than air gas. Individuals sublimate from the social structure as I retreat from its edge.

What becomes clearer than the content,
than the object of writing, is what
drove them to approach it this way.
Does knowing that give any control?
No, but it sure makes the
reader less receptive.

The smoke coming out of the stack,
the combustions below.
Another day, another alphabet.
A baby, an inheritance,
desire to resume, body against body, not
the talking distances power perpetuates.

I met a man who pleased me and I wanted to tell him but I had no words save those which seemed inappropriate, so I shuffled my feet and smiled down and went away, "comprising matrix, matter, and production all in one," only in relation to.
The crystalline past engenders a caress.
Such knowledge is a shield.
My love is coughing and can't stop.
I leave, remove,
split off one electron,
oust, auto da fé, goner.
I think this is the apocalypse.

"Even today government policies cannot be judged adequate, and
A bomb victims remain dissatisfied.

"The bombing of Hiroshima and Nagasaki resulted not only from a desire to end the war quickly and to restore peace; it came as we now know, from the US's expectation of a postwar confrontation with the Soviet Union and its wish to make a show of force by demonstrating the bomb's incredible might." But if one percent of mutations are favorable to the species, wouldn't a super race emerge from world holocaust with a more favorable population density than now, if a only new, low half life bomb could be developed....

ACCIDENTIALS

Talk about the power of the atom. All hate all fear all death all sex is in the word.
—William Burroughs

Here is real gastrointestinal chutzpa. He's got enough built up brownie points to survive his first brush with the reaper, but he won't get far. He's got no investment tax credits, he's got no names, he's got shit. What happens to a bum like that, a divested, nameless do-gooder. Why ding dongs swarm all over him at the first checkpoint. He will be submerged in a flaming pit of insurance forms, where his soul will be utterly consumed and destroyed forever while others with intact mummies and the right names to drop in the right places...O Billy, how could you treat me this way. I loved you so.

Flying ships, powered by bureaucracy, defenseless from paperwork, hang below a fretwork of retorts. The juggernaut runs without a hitch, personnel Rip Van Winkled by paronomastic conceits? (The continuing occurrence of the weedy cereal in tuber swiddens probably led to selective breeding.) Graceland snubbed his way through the ankle-deep dust.

Pushing open the door he sweated as depression ballooned out at him from the semi dark room. Everywhere realism was attempted by copying nature, but it was method not the copy that counted. The interested parties look over his shoulder, gaining time for one more round of matching quips for ego.

Thus, in art circles the question often asked, "Is there a species proclivity to lump plastic and metal or is it a post nuclear mutation," can't be answered from here. (The impotence of elite burial sites, such as the spire just inland from Chesapeake Bay, to inspire optimism about our past inclines archaeologists to hypothesize the dread Cult of the Individual.

Yet I increasingly feel the need to add, outside the boundaries of the exposed form, a stroke that makes the rounds of the conventions, splitting your infinitives in the name of freedom, of speech breaking down your windows or the spectacles in your eyes in a dawn cathedral, a holy war against entertaining facts.) Be reasonable, they counseled.

At the gate of the city, Graceland looked into pigeons. He was asked to pick a card. All the cards were the same. Doing what they asked he pointed out the futility of choice. “We try to remain contented here,” he was told, as they presented him with a bottle of the local vintage, Mouton Panurge. (The circulation of intelligence is really the circulation of spontaneous life. To promulgate intelligence, to misinform, is to control.)

Sick and tired of being controlled, he looked for mistakes to attract his abandon. (What seems surprising is that the discussion remains largely within such unaltered perceptual confines.) When metallurgy defines the beginning of civilization, make her be silent becomes the tax.

LIVE ACTION LANGUAGE

On the skin of burnt children,
There sheens a side of debit that if,
Of if about some of them,
15 miles from Times Square
There is a home for charity."
–American Enterprise Institute

In the grammatical arsenal,
which part of speech is strategic
weaponry? The nuclear threat
of an article or tense for form
or decoration is how it distracts
workers from the pursuit
of goal oriented problem solving.
Is the strength of their
desire questionable?
Should art threaten it?
Because one must always question
oneself first?

And the goal, pole, feint,
angularity of the artist, explorer, athlete, zealot?
The article or apostrophe placed
for pace is obliterated.
And then it's reprised.

(Our nuclear heritage is propelled by women, since the dangling participles don't want to be implicated in a joke.)

I the last (or the first) man
Am made to resemble a canned ham
by being placed on a tower with no power
by the centralized cajolery of the chiefdom
that succors those Parisian Hooples in our Necropolis.
A hybridized people quickly settles down to the kind of variation normal to any population.

Whether ancestral strains continue to manifest themselves in individuals remains a question.

(Does the writer have a voice or a voicing?)

The war started when evolutionists learned that traits were not transmitted over time through a large population and hence that their notions of quality assurance were distinctly weaker in mass formations. A small group of them decided to do something about that. They did, of course, as we now know, succeed. (The clouds of individuals overlap in the discriminate spaces. Short faced people, for example, will be assumed to be happy.)

These events, viewed from the bridge, appear tiny, sordid enough to make a soap opera seem dramatic from an ironing board. They crammed all the corner's dust into a moment of panic. (And I have here included the by now famous graffito, "Dyslexics of the world untie.") Expectation alone was enough to ruin Wednesday, the day before the bombing of our city.

Each time I remember then, I am torn alternately by a disgust for the mediocrity of my lives and an intolerable nostalgia for the fecundity and gentleness of a planet where the rain fell bearing vitamins. And with even greater clarity are etched the images of my fellow citizens going about their business, caught as by the passive voice at the moment of the unannounced explosion

A well dressed black man bends over to return a quarter to an elderly woman dressed in a fox fur stole who has dropped it while fishing for change to buy a newspaper whose headlines assure her of the gallant efforts of the peace negotiations team.

A lady of the day.

A man with a full beard wanders down an aisle of cubicles looking for a pencil.

A child from the Brahmaputra suture wide eyed presses his nose between the cheeks of a carriage horse.

A lawyer seeing death all around him decides that the only way to calm his fears is to face them and kill. He is waiting outside the president's office before being sworn in as the Minister of Terrorism and Culture when there is a blinding flash. Views of passengers slap happy on the platform and inside the train. Multiples framed by the subway windows, each spotlight on each face differently implying its own route of red tile commuter shoes.

(Brought to the sacrificial alter, Iphigenia welcomes her chance to serve.)

A paunchy middle aged woman in tight stretch pants walks her toy poodle into the oncoming fireball assuring herself that it's only a side effect of increased lithium dosage.

A man in a checked suit at a phone booth calls a number and, not getting through, calls the right number, but it's the wrong number.

The upper crust junkie, seeing her Puerto Rican lover across Union Square, mutters "Santa Maria" as the air raid sirens begin to whine.

A window washer, strapped to the twentieth story of a New Jersey office building, tears up his lottery ticket as the sill beneath his boots begins to shake.

A Korean greengrocer on Long Island sees a large mushroom reflected in the apple he is polishing.

Moira counts her blessings.

The organized crime figure's face is shoved into his chauffeur's crotch as the first shock throws him out of the black limo parked in front of the USDA's office.

The poet is really angry that she can't take her beer cans back to the bodega.

The arbitrageur waited too long.

I had the sense that I was remembering these events and not making them up to glorify myself with the imagined breadth of my experience and perfection of my values so vivid were they that I wanted to have already known them but could not be sure that I had "been there before" even in my most midnight mind, so obscure had my reasons for doing anything become in order to purge myself of values that seemed to me to be the chief cause of misery and pain and among these I include “mercy, pity, and peace.”

Art Is Pop Art

All eight sinus cavities,
Carrying strength and energy
To every part of your body.
Look, up in the sky.

EXCESS SUBTLETIES

"Will you be my little geranium,
Until we are both blown up by uranium."
— Bob Hope

When Carpaccio brought his father's tie out of the cardboard box he'd packed it in a few days after the funeral, his wife whaled into him. "You're always trying to confront people in a way they can't respond to. And then confusion poisons their response so you never relate to people. You only demand they relate to you, which, take it from me, isn't really that exciting only complicated by your motives.

"Of course, the reason you do that is because you feel like Dorothy in the tornado in the house with everything rushing by and nowhere to go but down." She stamped out of the room.

Carpaccio stood in front of the mirror and pulled the tie through his collar, sawing back and forth as he watch his Adam's apple twitch and sniffed the soap of his shave. As he knotted the half Windsor he reexamined the tie.

It was dark red with white, yellow, and bluish mushrooms printed on it or was it hand painted. What'd he know. He recognized porcini, amanita muscaria, and shitake and there were several he'd have to look up at the library. Up near the knot at first partly obscured but coming into focus as he drew the knot tight was a yellow and blue mushroom cloud. He could wear it. He'd wear it.

NUKEMAN

ABOUT FACE

Studying to attack the enemy, how their minds work:

Self serving propaganda and shows of force are effects
Which can be variously achieved. And certainly,
We should look good to be thought well of.

But the accessible arsenal and mobile strike team can be
Distinguished from even rows of missiles in a parade
And hollow displays of technology.

Rigorous training, war game corrections, and revising strategy
And tactics spark the insight to curtail defective force.

"Nukeman" introduces active considerations to the models
Of our nuclear heritage, tracing the confluences of war and art.

When fighting to make a living at the expense of others,
Different disciplines branch directly from our duties.

I have found multiple solutions
To a puzzle expected to have one answer.

Each soldier seeks a new conquest.

BOOT CAMP

Poetry stands in the margin contemplating the edge,
Drawing violence from memory and culture.
Assessing economic / natural cycles,
Poetry applies the innate solutions.
Assuming correctability, it seeks to control habitat and humanity.

Leaves torn away by autumn define the tree's cycle;

Tender buds of spring open for exploitation.
Winter frost brings an opportunity
For organizing, summer days for foray.

Our nuclear heritage relies on turning points of history
To define clarity and purpose, since it has become that way.

Our nuclear heritage valorizes the conflicts of the classic battles
Where form and content can be distinguished.

FIRST FORAY

Daydreams, he hears an inner "Taps".
His stealth bombers ride currents
In the four corners as his mind,
"Over the horizon", surveys.

And then intelligence clarifies bogeys.

And missiles pour forth, the shape of death,
Issuing particulate bitterness.

He drifts in a lake of reports;
He drives to the depths
Of weather radar, through drifting clouds of gasses.

And he scoops living beings, like fishes
Hooked in their gills, into his net of survivors.

And he brings down order like a duck
The buckshot bounced off;
Then it rises again.

And he gathers words and images
From anonymous hacked generations;
His rhetoric comes from Georgics millennia past.
And morning does not come,
For here is history known by no one, only light unfolds.

Past and present solute.
The earth was the blink of an eye.

SELECTIVE SERVICE

He chooses among assaults, his troops.
He appropriates tactics and crafts his 5th column,
Tracing echoes to their sources sonar, radar, laser, maser.

Following a branch to find the trembling recruit or a stream
To find the spring, the strategist brings light to the darkness,
Even if it means what's simple becomes difficult
Or the difficult easy.

So, battle tanks silence other guns, and heat seeking SAMs
Chase planes in terrifying waves away from the front.

In anabasis, the way is often cleared by artillery
But often the enemy is snide and regroups.

He calms his anxious generals;
All things mold to his strategies.

He collects from academy curricula proper battle assignments;
Sky and earth are trapped in his subterfuge.

Caught at first in a web of alternatives,
Now casualties aid his route.

Battle logic is the bone;
Tactical nukes make the appendages wave.

Emotion and reason unite and every shift
Of feeling calls forth fresh troops.
Finding rage, he also finds rage's tears;
In exultation a terrible sneeze.

Sometimes orders come easily,
Sometimes he sits and eats beef.

SATISFACTION

So recruits do not dispute,
The victor's pleasure beats rock star's.

Out of events identity licks,
Out of closets war cries justify his need.

Cast the net of fright wide wider.
Language trickles from particular connections in the brain.

The warrior spreads the fragrance
In an abundance of sprouting arteries.

Harrowing winds lift up the metaphor;
Clouds rise from a forest of history writing turrets.

CATALOG OF WEAPONS SYSTEMS

The body of suffering takes a thousand forms
With no right way to measure.

Human life changes at the flick of a hand,
The soul difficult to capture.

Squadrons and flotillas compete with the will
Of the people through the gunner's objective.

Caught between the historian and the idealist,
The strategist struggles to win battles without compromising
His munitions, his supporters.
He departs from the canon, oversteps the accords in search
Of a victory that has not destroyed the value of his conquests.

If his strategies are muddled, he cannot succeed;
Only when the mind is clear can his gestures be noble:

The air force captures the emotions and controls the battle.
The army goes to its goal directly.
The navy masters the supply routes and trade.
The commandos are ready at a moment's notice.
The Seabees protect our own shores.
The submarines are untraceable.
The missiles strike if necessary with final devastation.
The satellites see far.
The intelligence units pass among the enemy and delve his mind.
The quartermaster's corps is orderly.
The lines of communications are their own form.
The pacification teams provide the basics for a defeated foe and innocent victims.
The propagandists turn their anger at the victor to disorder.
The government liaisons prevent interference.
The assassins do what must be done even close to home.

Although each service is different, each stands opposed to
Whatever enemy, and none grants the strategist license.

Action speaks from its reason,
Language from its use.

BALANCED FORMATIONS

Each assault assumes particular shape,
But only when alternative scenarios are plotted.

Sentinels for each force harmoniously battle
Toward a mutual understanding of how to attack.

Weapons mingle like colors in a kaleidoscope,
Each enhances the form.
Training is like opening a dam in a river during a drought.

But troops are capricious;
Discipline shouldn't try to mirror personality.

And without individual initiative,
Even dialectics is not enough to drive a tank.

CORRECTING ERRORS

Looking back, one finds errors of judgment,
Moral oversights and crime.
Anticipating adverse publicity, one seeks
A smooth transition that will not compromise the leaders
Or the people.

Distinguishing action from result,
Errors in judgment can be compensated,
Oversights can be covered up,
And crimes can be punished or privately banked.
Confuse them and everyone suffers,
Because the foundation of patriotism,
cause and effect, is questioned.

The general inspects his soldiers down to a single hair.

When corrections are precise,
Even politics can frankly control the people.

THE KEY

Technology may be reassuring
And the logic of an assault accurate,
But the target may be trivial.

What has come to fruition requires no additional dispute
Until war crimes' prosecution.

A bullet in the heart, a grenade in the crucial turbine;
Political boundaries must not end.

However the supply lines branch and spread,
They bristle with strategic nodes.

When polarity is curtailed,
One is saved the pains of correcting errors.

Prowess Initiative Surprise Victory

Weaving elaborate divisions on muddy roads,
The plan must move the heart
Like a squadron of fighters roaring overhead.

New ideas rhyme with current events.
The human spirit spills into the same blood as ancestors.

I gaze humbly at my medals; I wear them for my country.

BREAKFAST CHAMPIONS

Perhaps only a single warhead of a cluster will find its target;
Perhaps only one person's ideas will be disseminated.

Beating your breast and shouting causes friends to wince.
An assault with too many objectives achieves none.

Shoddy soldiering is an eyesore, always obvious
And cannot be the source of operations.

When the troops are not stirred to battle, but alienated
By arbitrary discipline, their minds wander uncontrolled.

When the sun glints off a well placed piece,
The enemy is cowed; the associations ricochet in their minds.

A youth with an creative assignment might follow paths of glory.
A frontal assault within a great strategy might win today.

CRITERIA

Sustainability:

When the strike is slack and has no follow up,
The rhythm falters. The soldier searches in the dark
For a friendly, but finding none; he calls
And then calls on God: no answer.
A single attack, however courageous, is no operation.

Hierarchy:

When the foray is all bravado
And the technology overwhelming,
No one will praise the victory.

When the commando mixes with the foot soldier,
The commando suffers.

One hears a single shot in the night.

Value:

Searching for policy, a leader may obscure
And personalize the common good.

Then his words harden, ramble,
And the people feel betrayed.

As with prime time tv, one detects music and harmony
But cannot identify the tasty product. It is too expensive
To buy or pay in defeat. So, battles continue.

Restraint:

Sometimes the smell of blood
Or a convincing argument seduces.

Vanity mushrooms self aggrandized images in your mind.

Especially in a good cause, such as the use of firing squads,
Just proportion must be observed.

Torture:

When an assault is free of confusion,
Although lunch may be bread and water,
The troops' rage is proscribed.
All your resources can be deployed
And still the effort lack effectiveness.

Finding Strategy:

Know when to push forward to new objectives
And when to back off and regroup;
When to use satellite reconnaissance
And when to rely on reports from the ground
Or scrutinize the dispatches for signs of unrest.
Know when sentence planning has not addressed
The syntax and when the bureaucracy
Cannot find appropriate disguises.
Know when to let strategy find you.

Even when the charge is blunt, the results must be telling;
Even when the assault is frontal, the troops must move smoothly.

He who laughs twice hears himself the second time.

Tactics can be modernized; a stream we muddy soon runs clear.

The mess cook cooks better meals when the troops are happy.
The misfit has something to grumble about
Even when victory is at hand.
Common sense alone will not tell you how to strategize
And the journalists cannot describe it.

THE HISTORIC VICTORY

I press these rules of war to my heart
As I write rejections for draft exemption.

I know what's only fashion;
I remember what Caesar praised.

As finite as death seems,
Great deeds illuminate humanity's trajectory.
Yet such heroics remain opaque and magnetic,
While the dogface routine is a matter of records gathering dust.

We go to Congress, but our coffers seem ever empty.
The flashy, fundable proposals are like workers without jobs.
Wanting each new weapons system to be funded,
One supply general gets an ulcer while another plays golf.

Nothing remains perfect; the soldier is never complacent.

We hear the laughter of college boys and think they laugh at us.
The retreating commander continually counts his troops,
Thinking it will delay his own demise.

THE TERROR

I worry my victories have been misrepresented,
And another has seized the strategic objective.
Unworthy to lead modern vessels of power,
I want to initiate the Long March.

I work with materials at hand;
That which is over cannot be delayed.
Then the enemy shot six times rises.

The need for a particular action passes.
But its effects return as useful as an echo from Thermopylae.

When spring arrives, the troop's blood stirs
And public information encourages emotions.

Yesterday teamwork, today standardization.
Every eye sees the pattern,
And it don't take Alexander to hear the music.

INSPIRATION

Time comes when the armor is mired,
Though every order wants to be obeyed,
When individual initiatives fail.

The Campaigner feels dry as last year's pop star's facelift,
Dead as last year's pop star, as culture that feeds on nostalgia.

Wishing on his venture, he searches his self for a dream.
He relies on circumstances or the weather to change.
He scans the horizon for a convenient opponent.

The real victory is in the dark, strategies brought gently
Like a child from the womb, terrified and screaming.

Forcing actions forces errors;
Letting time take its course makes the course clear.

Victory lies in individuals acting in common cause
On multiple fronts, but no power on earth guarantees alliances.

Again and again, I search my heart in the struggle;
Sometimes another theater appears when I least expect.

An empire keeps a lasting peace.

ARMISTICE

Consider the use of force civilization requires.
Although all cultures want to rise above it,
As if the fetus could have no placenta,
They have not understood its limits.

The works of the "mighty crumble,"
Yet continue to be the goal of many
And the sonnet of laughter in peace and
And of sorrow in war.

Each generation is fathered by the military of the prior;
Only isolated tribes have no apparent pecking order.

The discipline of war makes leaders for peace
And illuminates moral questions.

War is like art because it must deal with calibrated spaces
And the conflicts of partisans.

War comes like lighting from the sky and claws the spirit.

Inscribed on bronze and marble, it is honored as virtue,
But every day must be today
And we must live on in our memories.

Based on the writing manual Wen Fu *by Lu Chi, ca. 300 CE*

Four For

1995

OLD AND NEW BE(E)N

Who shall doubt, Donne, where I a poet be,
When I dare send my epigrams to thee?
—Ben Jonson

I don't have to have sung
the 'plaint that's been sung by Old Ben
On My First Daughter and On My First Son,
because I have been with new Ben,
But sinned like the ancient then,
who hoped too much of the child of his right hand,
who to Donne did don a fawning cloak,
like I to our own Donne did,
mistaking homage paid occasionally like dues
Instead of constantly like breath or blood
or the tax of that has-been,
while his cat's paw on the back
of the neck affirms noblesse manque,
Who postures having been Dudley Do Right Do Wop:
a perfect temper for students
who only have to say as long as old Ben's Ben
and then depart with a bad taste of culture
to their engineering or proliferate these masks.

Accusative rapacity if you refuse collaboration,
heads up, look down legal whiplash
into the steel-drum sunrise of the garment refectory,
the sweet sweat shop
of don't even think of parking here.
Is there not enough to know
in poetry that I have to look elsewhere?

Fetal explorers and fecal exporters dance
across the printed lawn, while Yugoslavia,
test-tube baby of colonial machines, expires.
Spare it its well-meanuing advisors

and nationalists propounding liberty
when they merely mean to switch
control to themselves. Leaders will await
the fresh breeze die, then the old hoarse voice-
over will creep in, one that has been
awhile leering through the dream of freedom,
the Yugos that appeared courtesy of the Community.

While Ben be born, bear up to the older conflicts.
Literal is symbolic and not an objective condition,
blood and body and earth, what's been and done.
Among the abuses of metaphor,
that rehash of simplification employed against you:
the state exists for arguments between its citizens.

We proceed, jealous children chasing bright tears,
agreeing until it is too late and our force is lost,
or fighting until it is too late and the well has dried.

The main breeders and reactors are manifest,
but who should remember, also serve and teach,
interest clarifies in the lesser work.
The masters are concealers of their fate.

JALOUSIE, ROLLING STONES SECTION

What time can accomplish, reason can too.
—Anonymous

In the workaday world I reorganize businesses to make them more efficient by changing power structures within corporate or other divisional domains. When the officers begin to feel the pinch they yell as much as poets who find their language, over indulgent pater familias or Ea he or she is, priorities reorganized by abusive upstarts such as you might be. In fact why don't we eliminate every poetic vestige in poetry to make poetry.

But when I proposed to the good Dr. P that I was trying to decide if I was well enough to rea, he suggested getting deeper into my own mind, to reorganize my poetry; he suggested playing the poet, the long-sufferer, and to play it to the hilt. "Consider being a character in Magic Mountain because of your long suffering back and you'll fit the part." And so I reorganized the thought:
No fucking neurasthenia this ain't.

This immoral line has a double negative and as such would be ungrammatical in most writer's hands, but what if I think of the negative as being a two-part construction as the French ne/pas. The first no is no and 2nd no is me saying it.
This ain't no neurasthenia.

But you reply this is prose jargon. Authenticity as poverty of expression. Not elevating like poetry. That's why I say,
No fucking neurasthenia this ain't.

But when ain't no fucking neurasthenia.
No fucking neurasthenia this ain't this back.

Yes, it's me and I repeat this, building a poetic sentence from the twinges of form. But
This ain't this back

Alone sounds like "it is not this back" mine, of which I speak. Which is how doubling emphasizes and deflects. It's that I want to be the baby.

Meanwhile, if you remember, the snow continues to fall on Magic Mountain.
Time passing slower taken boring hour to boring hour, the years from repetition
of hours slipping by like snowflakes. The poet thrashing.
No fucking neurasthenia this ain't this back, it's my baby.

Note the jump from "my back is hurting to get attention" to" "this is my baby".
That's a poetic tradition: personification, metaphor, deflection.
No fucking neurasthenia this ain't
this back, it's my baby, no, no, no

Further deflection: baby to rock song. I want it to go away but I'm not sure who
I am addressing anymore, not who but it perhaps, addressing structures.
No fucking neurasthenia this ain't
this back, it's my baby, no, no, no
Back to my baby.

Now it's beginning to look like the other poems of this series.
Back to my baby strewing while Yugoslavia stews.

This Vita Nuova reverts again to wanting to be the baby and so back to the back.
No fucking neurasthenia this ain't
this back, it's my baby, no, no, no
Back to my baby strewing while Yugoslavia stews.
No, no, no. I want to be the baby,
So my back is no, no, no not neurasthenia.

OOPS!

2000-2013

THE CENSUS OF THE FISHES

Mr. A.
decided to count all the fish in the sea,
because he wanted to....
He went to the New England Fishermen's Association and said,
"I am going to perform a census of the fishes."

"Don't do that," said the Fishers, "the government will regulate what we catch. We won't be able to catch the fish that we catch today."

Mr. A. decided that he would find a more friendly reception among environmental groups. "Can you imagine," said Mr. A. to the Environmentalists, "that in 1992 we still do not know the number and composition of marine life? Wouldn't you like to know about

millions of fish,
billions of crustaceans,
trillions of krill,
and a quintillion of copepods?"

"No, we would not," said the Environmentalists. "As soon as you identify the populations, the Fishers will exploit them."

Mr. A. decided that there must be a premium on ignorance, so he went to the Cold War Scientists who were out of work, because the submarines no longer flowed from Murmansk. He said, "You have been counting submarines for 50 years, how would you like to count fishes?"

"We are concerned with opacity," they said. "We can treat each fish like a submarine with a distinctive shape and acoustic signature. With the end of the Cold War, technologies developed for looking for submarines are now available for other purposes, and at a reduced cost. We can attach a line behind a boat. It will trail the boat in a sine wave counting all the submarines, er, fishes you wish. We can count the shallow and deep all over the world.

"For years we have been writing algorithms to push the fish into the background and bring out the submarines. Now we can push the submarines in the background and bring out the fish."

Mr. A. felt relieved and reassured.

Note: the census of marine life was completed in 2010.

A FISH IN THE LOBBY OF 93 WALL STREET

So what is important,
if the universe decides not to challenge us, and even
breakwaters fall asleep?
Why, the old, seminal
undertow, that's what. The nor'easter will be out in force
tomorrow,
an insane force in an otherwise docile universe.
—John Ashbery, *Girls on the Run*

During the winter of 1993, the old wharf areas of lower Manhattan were flooded by a storm. As high tide approached, the East River rose to the level the Dutch found it in the early seventeenth century. For a moment, the news was filled with the news.

I was working in the financial district late that night. Leaving the office into a crowded rain, I noticed a curious light emanating from one of the buildings. I crossed the street and walked right to the edge of the incoming tide. As it lapped forward, I stepped back.

I looked into the glass and steel lobby at 95 Wall Street. The flood had swept into the tiled, sunken lobby, filling it with salt water, and a few large fish were swimming around as if they belonged there. I thought how strange that the fish did not appear to notice the change in their environment. How easily they adapted to the builder's structure, altering his purpose. Had the fish been part of a fountain or brought by the incoming tide? The water was rising fast.

When I got to higher ground on Broadway there was one cab. Another late-night worker viciously refused to share his ride with me, and I hastened home on foot in the driving rain, imagining the fish discussing the state of their affairs. And chiding myself for being bullied out of a taxi home.

Working in the financial district for twenty-five years one gets to thinking about alternatives. My first effort at environmental taxonomy layered one idea on another mimicking time.

NICHES

[W]hen an ecologist says 'there goes a badger,' he should include in his thoughts some definite idea

of the animal's place in the community to which it belongs, just as if he had said, 'there goes the vicar.'

—Charles Sutherland Elton, 1927

"Good Luck" Haiku
Crawls in a tunnel
That he made all by himself.
Poets meditate.
(don't other animals?
Each discrete organism
Independent and
Linked
In relational position.
That feels good, too.)
Subservient/subordinate/solvent
Allaying the words
A place with something in it
Or a place for something

Of poetic life—
an oxymoron.

I edited. Then I rewrote it.

"At a Certain Level" Haiku
The early bird picks
The above worm from the tunnel
They both inhabit.
Some letters are bigger than others
Specialized and generalized
They walk over
The snowy field
K-L-K-L-K

Analogy makes distinctions.
But risks fruitless relations

How can the rectangular page
Represent the pear-shaped planet?
How far beyond that
To the screens of psyche?
To think planet keep moving
But skin blocks the passage.

O
K
O
K
O
K
Thinking outside the head…
And I suddenly realized
It wasn't all about who…
Bug, bugger, buggiest
Give me a leaf quick
I gotta go expand
The firewall

To profess alternatively
It takes six weeks or more to heal.

The one and the other
They are unique but their cells:
Picaresque dentifrice.
Around the block with Mercator projections
Are the whole human experiment
Of only two sides.
More than feeding the cow:
A shape and other shapes,
More than the cry:
Fitting facts into another fiction.
What we put in overflows

And we don't clean up,
Leaving around and about.
The extra keeps its coffee grounds.
This and that
Creative residue.
Retract the valence,
But keep it handy.
Extend a hand:
"Cellular prosody"

Green is not enough.
Poetry is possible,
If we give it its head:
An anonymous flow job.

Extend myself to you.
Extend myself to me.
Extend ourselves.
Extend ourselves
In other directions.
The green hokey-pokey.

What do I think about that?
What do you think about that?
What do I make you think about that?
What do you think about that after I made you think it?
What do you think the next day?
And shifts too,
Another opportunity for dispersed light.
    A flamboyant cult awhile
    Then agnostic choices
    Remote host for the symbiotes:
    Her biceps.

What I said earlier
Is what I meant then.
  A flying squirrel, a flying gecko
  A flying elephant

Homologous
    Shared ancestry.
    Analogy: similar but independent
Anachronism deference.
    You'd like to say higher,
    But rather flatter.

Anyone
Arguments tried and tired
Linked and unlooping
Choker vines.

    An unrecognized threat
    A recognizable thread
Unintentionally irritating
Because elsewhere is easier.

What's wrong with a little assurance
About causality,
Even if we don't believe it?

    The left hand knows what
    The left hand is doing.

END

Niches, relational positioning, are incomplete in themselves, as are the species and groups of species in any geography… At least light, water, and standard atmosphere. They do not delve into any subject in aggressive specialization but together are intended to answer the questions more completely because the relationships are defined by the juxtaposition of the entities rather than following a single thread of argument which is a species of thought. I suppose I am valorizing a natural process over a human model of efficiency. I hope that readers will defer gratification, catharsis, and resolution to understand the value of a literature that reflects natural processes in a way that co-exists with human ones.

TAGMOSIS/PROSODY (CONNECTING PARATAXIS)

Discrete skeletal units are known as tagma. The process of fusion is called Tagmosis. Different patterns of skeletal tagmosis provide a primary criterion for identifying fossil arthropods.
—Stephen Jay Gould

Discrete structural units of poetry are known as prosody. The process of fusion of prosodic units is known as writing. Different patterns of prosody provide a primary criterion for identifying poetic affiliations.

Start with a bird in a tree.
See it: a thing, a fad, a need.

Two, three, four, and more starlings
Pack the black walnut.

Focus on the whole walnut, a green
Shape with black punctuation

That was recently starlings.
Concentrate on the whole copse:
A maple, an elm, a walnut. Honeysuckle,
Lilacs in sunny spaces bleed into the grass.

The landscape of things transforms
Into one of relations. Things lose
Their identity. Bonds compile
Into landscape. Words collect
Into blocks of paragraphs;
Disengage into masses of letters
And streams of space.

Phrases accrete into forms and thoughts,
Not one like a thing, but an
Interlocking and disassembling set.
Our inference machine connects
Facts and fuses

Them into theories. Our minds continue
To suppose segues and bridges
Between disciplines.

Juxtaposing prosody to tagmosis, for example,
Creates difficulties for political and ethical processes.
Politically, what thoughts can live together?
We assume relations of things
Proximate in trees,
Thanks to Linnaeus.
If we limit our perception
To the black starlings in the black walnut tree,
Specialized disciplines transform
Nature into objects for use.
Very practical. And our sense
Of self supports this supposition
To distinguish each from other
People, species and the landscape.

Ethically, which parts of ecosystems
Correspond to human constructs,
And where is human activity unique?
We constantly differentiate ourselves
When ego seems pertinent to survival.
We work in communities to build
Surplus to reduce risk. Thus
Community produces freedom?
Relational focus materializes emergent properties
That simulate imagination to formalize
Our production of poetry, biology, and community.

Parents teach ethics of cooperation.
From a comparison of human and primate
Societies, human groups nest
In more inclusive structures while
Primate societies are flat. Human families
Form by conjugal, monogamous partners,
"Remarkably unique" among primates.

Among most primates either males or females
Move to another group at puberty, "losing
Contact with their natal group permanently;
Dispersal is strongly sex-biased."
In humans either sex may stay or leave.
"Dispersed kin maintain lifetime bonds"

> Kin recognition is bilineal and of unparalleled
> Extent.... Humans maintain preferential bonds
> With their affines, or in-laws....a uniquely
> Human feature....close and distant affines
> Account for a large proportion of coresident
> Group members.... Instigating
> A state of mutual tolerance." Social awareness
> Leads to cooperation with non-kin,
> Regard for others, seeking
> Of linkages, cultural transmission,
> *(Hill et al., "Co-Residence Patterns in Hunter-Gatherer Societies Show Unique Human Social Structure" and Chapais "The Deep Social Structure of Humankind," Science (vol. 331 March 11, 2011, p 1276,7 &1286-89).*

And intolerance of deviant behavior.

Environmental interactions develop processes
Like a water cycle, a food chain,
A community of supporting individuals,
A supply chain that drives process efficiencies,
Interdisciplinary thought that overlooks/sees
What specialists appreciate as deistic details.

The conflict between things and connections
Arises when we as individual organisms
Revert to perceiving the world as a set of objects,
When multiplicity in societies or ecosystems
Threatens the individual objective condition. Hence we

Must build connectivity
Into the model of things

And isolate ideas to focus
On the organism.

Ego spotlights the self
In opposition to interaction,

Limits awareness of emergent properties.
Forcing behavior into an organism model

Reduces the value of interaction.
Can any construction hold these

Interactions, synergies and contractions?
Don't we sustain to build one?

How are these threads woven? The analogy
Between tagmosis, prosody, and ecosystem
Is a fine place to start, since data
And knowledge about them emerge
From process and relational thought
As well as from ontology. Tagmosis,
Prosody, and ecosystem identify a whole
Organism/poem/biosphere built of interacting
Components. None of the prosodic or skeletal
Units are really independent like a sentence
Or commensal bacteria. Therefore our limit
Condition entails sets of mostly dependent components.

Working with process enables us to see self-identified interactions. Working with ontology develops the temporal relationships of both the individual organism and its interactions. Process and ontology interoperate and need to acknowledge that they do so.

INTER-DIMENSIONAL UNIVERSALITY OF DYNAMIC INTERFACES

For Rob & Vanessa

A collaboration can reflect the personality of a single artist as it did in the studio of Rembrandt where, according to recent scholarship, t6he marks of the Master's most intimate subjectivity—brushstrokes, psychological insight, impasto, 'touch'—turn out6 to have been applied at times by hands other than his own. Thus, the one artist who has always been thought of as unique, as a particularly subjective kind of genius, seems to have engaged in a form of corporate art making.
—Susan Collins & Nina Castelli Sundell, *http://collabarts.org/?p=68*

- The remediation
  of climate change lies not in chemistry, legislation or poetry but in their relationships.
- Relationships may be of several kids from active bi-directional to uni-directional or passive links that are only energized under certain circumstances. Each of these types may be stronger or weaker depending on conditions.
- Competition and difference attract an inordinate amount of energy in the arts, sciences, and politics whereas symbiosis and similarity are far more ubiquitous.
- Survival drives awareness of difference, but if we focus on them we end up reasoning from the outliers. A model that keeps us aware of similarities and differences would help improve the value of diverse organisms and things.
- Environmentalism thrives on an active mutualism of human endeavors that use the contemporary components of each discipline to best effect. Non-human endeavors are similarly impacted.
- Effect is intended: this is not an aesthetic exercise taken in isolation.
- To stimulate a common global consciousness based on current conditions, environmental poetics engages current modes and methods of production focused on their trends.
- These modes and methods condition attitudes like practitioners developing works and styles supporting environmental values into the future: sustainability.
- These activities and values must be potent enough to provide humanity with the will to change from a species-centered culture focused on the individual to an environmental one focused on common responses of organisms of many species and their relationships.
- Environmentalism, while broadening the focus, maintains humane activity for human interactions. Contradictions are imposed across species to complicate

this task. As one of the political animals humans can pay close attention to how humane behavior can be achieved in an environmental framework.

- Environmental poetics must be flexible enough to change with related models in politics and science, and in some cases to lead that change.
- Politics and science can in their current forms propel remediation of the environment, but culture is wedded to past destructive and separatist tendencies between humanity and non-human components of the environment.
- As a structure, environmentalism must be flexible enough to change as conditions change and not be chained to a past idée fixe relying on natural pietism and devotion to nature that is opposed to humanness and become a means of control in the hands of highly productive individuals and their groups.
- As a set of practices environmental culture must allow multiple innovations in concept and execution to be included, rather than an exclusive group of prejudicial attitudes. Dominance of one group of attitudes may be inevitable but hopefully temporary.
- Such diversity accommodates ecosystems and their populations of humans and other species in multiple climates both seasonal and relatively constant.
- Change, however, comes from individual or team discoveries promoted initially by small groups.
- Environmental culture must be flexible enough to allow intense mono-culture as one group of diverse elements so that detailed professional work of the highest caliber can advance our understanding without distraction of countless environmental influences.
- The culture retains its structure and awareness to minimize the likelihood that an extremely successful and cogent mono-culture gain control of the diversified, distributed structure and limit future options.
- Diversity includes expansive as well as conservationist approaches to problems since excluding some of humanity's tendencies builds resistance to the main thrust of environmental diversity.
- Environmental diversity does not require consistency as nature is complete rather than consistent and often contains contradiction and duplication.
- Environmental poetics avoids dichotomous argument except where relevant. Rather it presents a matrix of roles and things as well as their moment to moment changes along changing conditions.
- The sentence unifies subject and predicate not by making a third thing but by suggesting their relationship as an entity. A true noun, an isolated thing, does not exist in our physical surroundings. It is a perception and a factor of mind.

- Environmental culture uses this matrix structure to further effect diversity and attitudes that support diversity in spite of the human tendency to see the world from an individual's perspective through the structure of self and other.
- Environmental culture will not be perfect, and is not yet complete, but seeks to stimulate responses in kind that can overtake the politicized arguments of much of current classical and popular culture.
- Environmental culture does seek to keep us focused on itself and the risks of change so that we continue to support its poetics/purpose.
- Environmental poetics establishes universal diversity without relying on internal consistency so that mono-culture and specialization can occur among species and individuals and functions of individuals.
- Environmental poetics models its cultural solutions on natural methods more than descriptions of nature.
- Description of nature, as in ecopoetics' new nature poetry, functions to promote environmental awareness as a general case of mind/body dualisms.
- Environmental poetics tends toward alignment with environmental structures in order to move humanity's culture into association with them, not identical to nature but aligned with and fitting into the appropriate niche for a dominant species that recognizes a level of interdependence with the other planetary components.
- While environmentalism begins with a concept of nature, in the end human and natural elements are coincidental. The definition of nature as distinct from humanity withers away, and we remain with a definition of nature as inherent characteristics, as in the phrase "it's his nature to behave in that way."
- Universal diversity raises questions about the exact value of difference.

Uttering the word universality raises objections from postmodern culture.

SNOWBALL EARTH CREATES INNOVATIVE POETRY

For the roads there are animals . . . "Where does this road go?"
—Rabelais

The intense focus on social life in cities by innovative writing during the past 250 years obscures the truism that human activity is not unnatural or separate from nature. People behave strangely, but we are still biological organisms. Our cognitive powers, while in many ways unusual, remain a product of natural selection.

In one respect, however, humanity distinguishes itself as a single species by threatening to significantly alter the climate of the entire planet and thereby cause the extinction of many if not most of earth's species. While exceptional we cannot really credit ourselves with being the first species to cause wholesale climate change. As long as a billion years ago, massive blue-green algae blooms produced enough free oxygen to drop the average temperature to around -500C. The planet iced over as deep as 1km on all oceans. Slowly volcanic activity raised CO2 levels and the planet returned to a habitable temperature. The receding glaciers fragmented earth's tectonic plates. This process may have occurred several times. In the "Evolution of the Marine Phosphate Reservoir" Noah Planavsky et. al. postulate that:

> *Specifically, there is a peak in phosphorus-to-iron ratios in Neoproterozoic iron formations dating from ~750 to ~635 Myr ago, indicating unusually high dissolved phosphate concentrations in the aftermath of widespread, low-latitude 'snowball Earth' glaciations. An enhanced postglacial phosphate flux would have caused high rates of primary productivity and organic carbon burial and a transition to more oxidizing conditions in the ocean and atmosphere. The snowball Earth glaciations and Neoproterozoic oxidation are both suggested as triggers for the evolution and radiation of metazoans. We propose that these two factors are intimately linked; a glacially induced nutrient surplus could have led to an increase in atmospheric oxygen, paving the way for the rise of metazoan life.*
>
> Nature 467, 1088–1090 (28 October 2010)

These speculations reveal that primitive algae conditioned the planet for advanced life forms. Given the immense time horizons imagination does not have to stretch far to foresee how human carbon emissions can tip the planet into a hot spell that would result in elimination of most species. Even if you do not believe these facts, even a modest risk that they might be true would encourage you to change your behavior. If algae can create conditions for life, certainly human ingenuity can destroy it.

Why then would we knowingly continue to behave in a way to destroy our habitat? Because individual organisms attempt to survive and propagate themselves until their condition changes. Life could not thrive if individual organisms did not seek to improve their chances of survival through territorial control, reduced use of energy to feed ourselves, forming groups and reproduction. Individuals and group formation will continue to overuse planetary resources until our collective willpower or external forces change. The biology of individual organisms drastically affects our species' ability to act on obvious facts and risks. We know how strongly people assert themselves.

Culture helps individuals to assert themselves. The delusion that the human ability to reflect helps us to control ourselves operates as the cultural isomorph of the organismal survival drive. This delusion continues to jeopardize our ability to understand what we're doing as a species. From Genesis to graphic novels and 21st century poetry, culture reinforces misapprehensions about the human ability to consciously govern our actions. How can we change culture to reinforce behavior that supports acting our collective interest?

Currently, innovative writing supports our myths about our uniqueness by attending increasingly to the materials of creation and presenting concrete themes in increasingly elaborate disguises. From social writing to psychological and personal narratives, to theaters of ideas, to the poem itself, and most recently to language-centered writing the materials of construction dominate literary imagination. As innovation progresses our perspective has become increasingly internal. At the same time writing addresses more subjects, apparently democratizing culture, but its structural complexity and underlying theory have the unintended side effect of excluding more and more readers from believing that contemporary writing has something important to tell us about how the world works.

And true to the biological tendency of each individual organism to act in its own interest, these excluded readers have developed independent forms and audiences, further marginalizing innovative writing. From the narratives of country music to graphic novels to movie and video games' solo male protagonists, the broader cultural picture has fragmented and reduced older forms such as poetry to specialized readership. We might view this progress toward popular culture as appropriate if we did not have the collective problems of population expansion and climate change hanging over our heads.

Innovative culture by failing to address more concrete issues and capture broader audiences abets the separation of human activity from other planetary agents. Fragmentation extends far beyond poetry to disconnected silos of knowledge in many fields of endeavor. We are taught to separate art from science and from politics in a way that justifies ignoring the environmental links between those vertical compartments and the synthesizing of ideas in all but the most pragmatic frameworks such as management, marketing, distribution, and accounting, contributing to the rise of corporate oligarchy unfettered by a sophisticated culture confronting its power.

Since corporate succor barely exists, reborn fundamentalisms within all major religions, New Age Culture, Asian styles of meditation, deep ecology, and Jungian synchronicity have arisen to soothe people's suffering. These cultural alternatives proliferate as the corporate drive toward specialization and focus on technical skill undermines the awareness of the environmental connectors that afford people confidence and a sense of well-being. While human welfare has been and continues to be the purpose of civilization, neither our cultures nor our leadership apparently promote it. Instead contemporary culture encourages complacency overlaying insecurity.

There are, nevertheless, some good reasons to accept these divisive boundaries between silos of thinking. (It's never simple unless you are economical with the truth.) Each discipline's independent tools help acquire detailed knowledge of and excellence in any field. (General knowledge is suspect for several reasons.) But once the valued distinctions have been established, what psychologists call the narcissism of small differences takes hold to fossilize the borders.

Artists and scientists often place colleagues' work into categories in order to dismiss it, attack it, or otherwise affirm their own existence in distinction to it. In essence, to categorize is to dispose of certain details in a way that distorts the complete picture of our artistic ecosystems. If a work cannot be categorized, it is easily marginalized as outsider art, dismissed as experimental or condescendingly referred to as quirky or personal.

This tyranny of taxonomy separates what is otherwise related among the different arts, between arts and sciences, between A and B. As a practical matter, resolving dilemmas and eliminating false polarities would be facilitated by the tree structure of biology that would help us to think about related poetries, related ideas, and related individuals simultaneously in both separate and common spaces. Of course we do that already, but I rarely represent the fact that I am both myself and part of my family when I discuss my poetry; it's not good for the career. I can and should represent myself as a writer who is part of several innovative poetic tendencies. But when I do that many of my fellow poets deride the connections, calling them schools as if working together somehow diminished my value as a writer. On the contrary, to encourage individual organisms to see collective reality would be a valuable artistic contribution.

The cultural entities that I simultaneously inhabit add to my effectiveness as well as to the depth of my work. Communities with an acceptable public identity would make public discussion of poetry more productive and less an evaluation of individual worth. (This is not an easy job, because differences are often far more stimulating than similarities, but more on that later.)

Another isomorph of focus on the individual: Isolation of the disciplines of learning and action from one another has allowed the rise of the marketplace model, the zero-sum competitive game of boutiques where everything is treated as if it were for sale. This model suggests that pursuit of self-interest in the aggregate produces results supportive of collective interests. Quite the opposite has proven to be the case in the example of the global financial system. Self-interest, both individually and unfettered in the aggregate, destroys the social fabric by creating confusion between individual necessities with collective values. The domination of exchange value and marketplace competition sadly extends to basic human needs like health care and education to the detriment of both. It extends even to the tiny, impoverished poetry world.

For example, the Lila Wallace Fund (*Reader's Digest*) offered money to literary publishers to build market-oriented strategies aimed at publishing books based on how well they can be distributed and sold. Publishers who accepted these grants were disposed to change their editorial stance to fit the requirements of the grant. Some succeeded but many excellent presses died of expansion. The market mentality justifies such transitions as creative destruction just as global destruction of species allowed the rise of more complex life forms. But do we want to be precursors to the next advance of life? Rather we'd like to improve and appreciate our species and those around us. A careful look at our pretexts might allow us to avoid what now seems like the inevitable demise of our species by our own hand. Changing course toward policies addressing collective interest would be an exciting example of rationality. How can environmentalism help us to move toward that goal?

One of the supporting pillars of individualism, specialization, and marketplace mentality, Descartes' views the mind as part of an organism where cognition takes place as if on a stage. The Cartesian metaphor dominates our culture of thinking even though it has been thoroughly questioned by several subsequent philosophers. While Descartes model of cognition supports the biological individual, it fails to address the collective social and species influences on our lives. Environmentalism can only become effective throughout our culture if we can develop an environmental model of cognition and replace the Cartesian metaphor and its personalized vision that sequesters all valuable thought within the individual. And it might do so in correct proportion between internal and external thinking.

In his article "Environmental Epistemology" (*Ethics & the Environment,* 10(2), 2005), Mark Rowlands, professor of philosophy at the University of Miami, suggests that cognition can be said to take place both inside the body and "also in the manipulation and transformation of external information-bearing structures." Several functions take place externally, especially the function of memory, like an external disk array on your computer. "In certain circumstances, acting upon external structures is a form of information processing."

Organisms exploit external resources in order to reduce their energy consumption and increase survival rates. Rowlands cites how a beaver's dam-building skills make food more accessible with less effort and less risk. The beaver might have developed longer legs and bigger muscles to run from the pond to the tree to eat its bark before the wolf could catch him. As an adaptation such a strategy would use far more energy than a strategy that manipulates the environment. Taking fewer risks, the beaver who adapts through manipulation of the environment survives more often than the physically enhanced beaver.

Recent conceptual poetry uses a related strategy, appropriating prior texts, recontextualizing them and publishing them largely unchanged. The success of new conceptual poetry, from the environmental point of view, must be focused on that low energy output / strong reader response conceptual poets' attain. Ironically, with little work applied conceptual poetry achieves a greater amount of consideration compared to poets laboring diligently on the page. And predictably many writers flock to utilize this low effort poetics.

In another example, a person finds spices on a shelf. Rather than memorize the position of each spice, the cook runs his forefinger across the bottles, reading the label on each bottle in turn until he finds the one he wants. Understanding the position of the bottle that he wants takes place both inside and outside the mind, creating a situation where cognition takes place.

> The cognitive operations, by way of which we are supposed to acquire information about, hence represent, the world, are themselves, at least in part, processes *of* the world. They possess, quite literally, worldly constituents. And even those vehicles that can legitimately be regarded as located inside the skin of cognizing organisms can, in many instances, not be *identified* independently of the world. Such vehicles will, in many instances and perhaps most, have been designed to operate only in conjunction with the *manipulation of environmental structures.*

This low-cost strategy makes it more likely that organisms survive in conditions of reduced resources. It also accounts for human success. The drive toward social structure in towns is a good example, although recently developed balance sheets of energy consumption raise questions about the efficacy of certain economies of scale. Our social organizations like cities and governments exemplify external cognition, and the fact that we build cities proves the inadequacy of an internal-only model of cognition to account for existing conditions.

Rowlands cites the case of the mobile, adolescent sea squirt that has developed a rudimentary brain that allows it to move about collecting food. In adulthood, to enable reproduction, it affixes itself to a rock and proceeds to eat its own brain as an energy-saving method. How often in my life have I applied only a few things that I know in order to get a job done and not confuse thinking with the execution of the task at hand?

The notion that cognition can take place as a complex combination of activities inside and outside the body helps explain why we need to be concerned about the condition of the environment. Establishing that self-interest includes the individual in the ecosystem extends the idea of environment to the mind itself. Linking internal and external processes by defining cognition in this way promotes environmentalism from the core of our being, not as an abstract, impersonal value that we ought to support. If we think of our surroundings and ourselves as integrated entities then we might stop using our environs as trash bins and develop increased respect for other people.

Externalized cognition represents a first and vital step toward environmental perspectives. Writing looked at this way becomes an example of such externalization. Interestingly, poetry dealing with the materials of writing, from Mallarme's *Le Livre* to Silliman's *The New Sentence,* includes a great range of external subjects and materials, expanding poetry from a few monolithic subjects like love and war to complex and multiple issues. These writing strategies that use diverse materials and practices open the door to an extended poetry that addresses real-world concerns. Such writing practice potentially reestablishes poetry as a valid knowledge-creating process. Focusing on culture this way reduces the limitations of innovative culture's narrowing focus on the materials of construction.

In *Cheerleader's Guide to the World: Council Book* (Roof, 2007), Stacy Doris constructs the work from internal and external components rather than by analyzing a core event or idea through internally consistent logic. The book "…sandwiches Popul Vuh Patterson/Tibetan Dead Jigme Linpa Pindar//Rah rah." (The quotation is followed by a chart of a football play as if drawn for a high school sports team.) "The good old idea//was that corn growth//+ tax cuts make leisure."

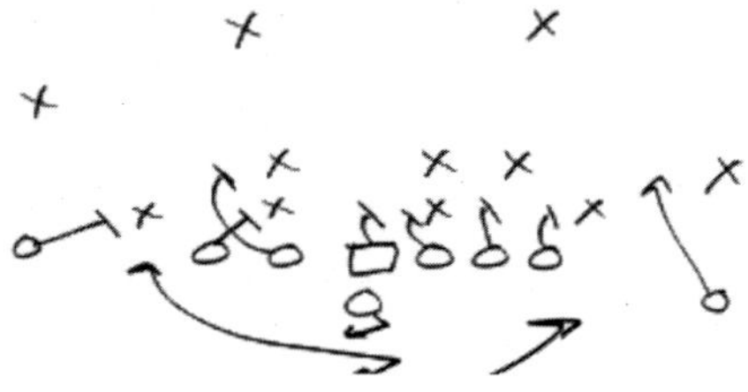

By juxtaposing these elements, Doris relates them physically on the page and establishes a variety of connections between internal and external components of varying strength and usefulness. Some of these associate subconsciously, some through our knowledge of history, and some through their inherent connections such as common content. In all cases, the exercise establishes a cognizant link of person and external components in an environment. These links reach out from the mind to the page and back. We read them again and they change; we are thinking as we read.

Compare Doris' lines to a sonnet by Milton where emanating from god "… thousands at his bidding speed / and post o'er land and ocean without rest…" all with the same interest, passively waiting to execute his will. While each differs, they agree on a common master. Here people outside the mind of god link only to god's will and the poem refers to the readers established understanding about biblical text. But even in Milton's case using fixed meaning the reader thinks using the words on the page as much as what is already in the readers mind. Milton's poem talks about internal cognition but is read using a combined process evident of external cognition.

Doris' synthesis reveals another kind of agreement. Synthetic poetry is greater than the sum of its parts, requiring more than the components of its construction to be read and absorbed. In this sense, poetry is externally understood. Meaning goes beyond the poem on the page to the experience and assumptions of the reader.

Like the beaver dam, Doris' synthetic poetry expands our access to resources that common usage would exclude. By juxtaposing the different texts, *Popul Vuh, Paterson,* etc. they arrive together in the present in the poem. Collapsing time represents one tool that writing uses to deliver cultural change and expand the possible solutions to our climate problem. By showing readers past, present and future together new correlations develop. But synthetic poetry requires more than juxtaposition to operate as an ecosystem.

Putting components together in an operative way, such as syntax for example, where their resources become available to each other creates examples for the poetic components to be guided by and push against as in any ecosystem, moving the metaphor into a reality that extends beyond that of a figure of speech. Poetic metaphor represents a real world analog of the complex interactions and correlations of components in the biosphere both symbiotically, homologically and experimentally such as using mice to help understand human disease. Mice and humans are not the same but have many similar processes. Accurate comparisons are few but in sufficient numbers to make many of Doris' combinations valuable culture modifiers.

What's human is formations
and drills. In the mix not the
matter or match. The commercial
habitat ploughed tracked stolen
or too glorified and thought
may be boating.
(*Cheerleader's*, p23)

Doris' combinations allow us to look at the components in a comparative way as they appear in the world rather than as they appear in their own context. Improving our skill in understanding the perspective of another context or another person's context will be important in addressing the multi-context view of global climate change. The combinations that Doris links are forms that enhance poetic technique much as rhyme makes poetic lines both more memorable and prosodically connected.

Localized technique used without reference to form, that is, not modeled, leads to a practice of poetry based on an invertebrate abstraction without understanding how that abstraction arises, that is, without analysis. Put another way, the more language is isolated from the forms where it is used, be they poetic, that is, multidirectional, or instrumental and toward a specific purpose, the more fixed meaning becomes. Fixed meaning in a limited context effectively accomplishes specific tasks, but does not allow us to think outside its context. Doris adapts the links to each context. Where they work, like genetic code, we achieve poetic lift off. Where they don't work, the writing falls flat.

Environmental poetics provides analytic models such as externalized cognition that can perform many functions in support of synthetic writing, addressing multiple contexts and actually understanding another person's point of view. It provides tools and connectors for poetic components as well as a well-documented history of how those techniques have already been applied. And consistent with the practice of environmental poetics, examples from biology display the values of models in poetry. (This book is intended to be not just an argument for its idea but also an example of it.) Metaphor viewed as an example of complex systems also appears as a useful tool and I see no reason to avoid such extended metaphor or its use in modeling.

Metaphor as Taxonomy
Grasping this as that,
More than a thing
Of beauty. Instead a bond
Of scales, cleaving
To poetry. Dialing
The iris risks ungrammatical
Acts, but riskless verse
Sings alone in the shower.
Metaphor more than
A fig leaf of speech
Represents the world
Where each shares
Enough of another
To be called a part.

Alas metaphor also makes it difficult to maintain a serious mien about this process of environmental poetry and its ridiculous appearance. Using examples from biology to validate literary arguments, describing poetry in such grandiose terms—these and many other methods used in the book have often made me laugh at myself while writing. To stop using nature as a person, but instead limiting the definition of nature to intrinsic characteristics supports such a physical universe.

But irony at many levels also plays a part in negotiating the change from a walled topography to a geography of permeable membranes within an organism. Just how seriously can we take this approach? Can irony exist at a continuous level in an environmental text or is it always modified by the reader's relation to what she is reading? Can we show the value to the environment of irony, which has heretofore been largely an aesthetic technique or approach to social criticism?

As we begin to distribute the environmental model, we also will need a new social taxonomy to replace the one observed by Chaucer in *Canterbury Tales* at the dawn of humanism and that is still in operation. As people begin to assimilate the environmental view, how will they be reorganized? How will they interact? What kinds of institutions will replace the existing ones, which are based on prior, polarized models? We could wish for no more than a suspension of time. Let us go forward.

An earlier version of this piece was published in ecopoetics journal #2, *ed. Jonathan Skinner. The original title was "Environmental Poetics" which became the subtitle of the first book of essays.*

THE WORLD TRADE CENTER ENVIRONMENT STRATEGIC DIALOGUE

UHF Tower Mast A
VHF Main Antenna Bracing, Southeast
Left Rear Wheel Assembly, Retractor
Random Array
First Class Galley Convection Oven Number One
First Class Galley Convection Oven Number Two
— Michael Gottlieb, "*The Dust*"

Dialog(ue) in a Dust Cloud

I was within two blocks of the WTC on September 11, 2001, in my cubicle in the Federal Reserve Building on Nassau Street on a conference call when the first plane hit, and I thought, "Someone is trying to stop the Wall Street opening." (It has happened twice in the past few years that bombs have gone off in the neighborhood just before 9 A.M.) When the second plane hit, it was much louder and the building shook. I said to my callers, "I think something bad is happening; I have to go."

I went to the window, and I could see the WTC burning. I watched in a state of denial as women fell, their dresses ineffectual parachutes. I thought, "I will just go back to my desk and get some work done." Then the first building collapsed, as time had collapsed. I could see it falling toward me and raced behind a pillar at the far corner of the office. (At the same moment my son, Ben, was racing away from his school on Greenwich Street and later described how, from his vantage point looking south, "the top of the building just slid off.")

Then we were benighted by a gray dust cloud, unable to see out the windows although the air was secure in the building. After 20 minutes the dust settled, and we could see out the windows again. Security evacuated the building; the Federal Reserve employees went across the street to their bunker in the bank; the rest of us dispersed. As I passed Beekman Hospital on William Street, the second building collapsed. I could see the dust cloud billowing toward me over the rooftops. I ducked into Pace University to avoid the dust cloud that slammed the door behind me.

For 20 minutes, I sat in the basement auditorium with a professor of African history, and we discussed the state of Islam. After exchanging credentials, the professor said, "I wonder why the sub-Saharan African leaders haven't been more supportive of the jihad."

"There's a difference," I replied, "between religious devotion and self-interest."

We in New York have suffered a great deal in the past few weeks. The military, financial control, surveillance, and charitable work of our government are a complex response to a singular, traumatic, personal attack on the financial center of our global commercial empire. But it's not about us.

Islamic militants are attacking us, to be sure, but their goal is to use us, and our expected inappropriate response, to destabilize secular, Middle Eastern governments and replace them with Islamic regimes.

Originally published in full in Chain 9 *eds. Juliana Spahr & Jena Osman, 2002.*

APPENDIX B: SCENES FROM FALLEN ARCHES: A MYSTERY PLAY IN EDEN

This compost.
—Jed Rasula

Characters:

Giraffe: Good-natured optimistic beast
Sheep: Sheep
Skunk: Self-destructive critic
Dodo: Purist
Adam: The First Man
Eve: The First Woman
Devil: Fallen Angel
Snake: Scapegoat with no legs
Gabriel: Messenger of God

Act I

Scene 1: The Garden (music: "The Hucklebuck")

Giraffe: I don't know.
Sheep: Beats me.
Skunk: What to do; what to do.
Giraffe: I don't know.
Sheep: I don't know.
Skunk: I don't know.
Giraffe: Beats me.
Sheep: Beats me.
Skunk: Beats me.
Giraffe: What to do; what to do.
Sheep: What to do; what to do.
Skunk: What to do; what to do.

Scene 2: The Audience

Giraffe: Get your hot programs here. I've got hot pabulum here. I am a hot pogrom here.

Skunk: Get lost lady. Let an experienced hand do the job.

Giraffe: Ok, big boy, but don't bend it all out of shape.

Skunk: These are your hot programs. All the programming you want in one program.

Sheep: Honey, you stink at this. Let me try.

Skunk: Don't tell me what to do.

Sheep: I'm a wooly prognosticator, I tell and don't tell.

Skunk: Here! I didn't want to preach the rates anyway.

Sheep: Whatever you want here. You name it and this is it. Your whole desire cranked into this flyer. Here's the info on what you need, where you need it, and when. A whatever you think it is infobot selected to be yours by me from among all I could think of without being anything at all except this.

Devil: Isn't that a little far-fetched?

Sheep: It's really the way it is.

Devil: I beg your pardon.

Sheep: Reminds me of my first trick, I mean caper, I mean gambol when I was told what to do.

Devil: I bet you didn't want to.

Sheep: I'll take that wager and the money that goes with it. I wanted to, you bet honey bunch, but I wanted to on my own terms.

Devil: What terms are those?

Sheep: I let you watch and you pay me to do it.

Devil: You'd better be good.

Sheep: I give you what you need.

Devil: If I'm paying I get what I want.

Sheep: You don't anywhere else. You buy the dishwasher as is. Why should an artiste, such as myself, be forced into servitude to your vulgar tastes?

Devil: Because they made the dishwasher for me.

Sheep: That's what they say.

Devil: Now that you mention it....

Sheep: At least an artiste, such as myself, I might add,

expresses her inner life and satisfies herself about quality. At best she changes the way we think. And we know quality assurance in the arts is a big thing these days.

Devil: I got what you need, babe.

Sheep: Save the macho crap for someone else, bozo. (Exit Devil in a huff.) I told you I had the goods.

Skunk: Some goods are not as good as others.

Sheep: Stop evaluating.

Skunk: I can't.

Sheep: (Aside) He doesn't know what's good for him.

Scene 3: The Garden (music: "Amazing Grace")

Giraffe: He is one of us. He is one of us.

Skunk: Not that I can see. He is a two-legs.

Dodo: And what do you see here? I mean what's below this toupee? Can you count?

Skunk: 1,2,3,4,

Dodo: I mean count my legs and divide by two.

Skunk: No offense, but you don't count.

Dodo: Sure I do. One, two, three, ha!

Skunk: And that's the proof about two legs. They are not born inferior, but being born with two legs they develop unstable behavior.

Giraffe: Certainly it must be open to question.

Skunk: It is a question why we don't just get rid of them.

Giraffe: They are born animals like us. They drink milk from their mother's breast. They beat their chest when they are threatened. There is no proof that they shouldn't get equal rights with all the other animals, assuming they survive the test.

Skunk: Gravity is just too much for them and their nerves fray as they learn to walk. What other animal has to be taught to walk? Human culture is shaped by the genes. And their belief in god is a survival instinct.

Giraffe: And are their genes shaped by their culture? Darwin said there's no feedback. The mechanism either works or gets whacked out. I mean look at who's talking.

Sheep: Boys, boys. Calm down. God is infinite and dismal. We must allow his plan to work. Even though it bores us, we cannot interfere.

Skunk: Just follow along, right to the slaughter. How'd you like to follow this. (Exit smelling)

Sheep: What a gas.

Giraffe: I'll keep above this one. (Exit)

Scene 4: Naming the Animals: A Rehearsal

Adam: Lemme see. You look like a sheep. I call you sheep.

Sheep: Lots of luck, big boy.

Adam: Wow, what can we call this one?

Eve: I'm not the taxonomist around here.

Adam: I'll call you nectarine.

Giraffe: You want to saddle me with a name like that. Everyone'll say, "Look at the neck on that nectarine."

Adam: I didn't saddle you with anything; you're not a horse; a horse is a horse of course; and you're not one. You are what you are and you're a nectarine.

Eve: Adam, darling, maybe she's right about the neck thing.

Giraffe: Well, I suppose it's ok to be a nectarine, but I wasn't one when we started this conversation, you know; you made me one. You keep saying I am one, but...

Adam: What's the big deal? Either you are one or you aren't one. And since I say you're one, you're one.

Eve: Just a second. It says here under nectarine, a smooth-skinned variety of peach.

Sheep: That's what you said to me last night, Adam.

Adam: Shut up. Drat. Well, if it can't be a nectarine, what can it be. Nobody appreciates my work here.

Eve: Don't get all testy, darling. What we're doing here is naming the animals. You don't have to name them all yourself. Why don't you let this one choose its own name.

Adam: Can't do that, sweetie dumpling. If I let this one choose its own name, they'll all want the privilege. And then if we get two animals wanting to be called Lion, then I'll get a discrimination lawsuit from the one who chose second.

Eve: Ok, if you have to make all the decisions then you can't object when you contradict yourself. It's your own fault.

Adam: OK OK OK OK OK OK OK. What do you want to be?

Giraffe: Oh, I don't know, let me see. I see, I see a beautiful long-necked creature enamored of leaves high up in the beautiful trees.

Adam: Be not see. We all see you, and quite a sight it is. What do you want to be. Be, be, be.

Eve: Bee, a winged insect...

Adam: Pulease, do you have to.... Beauty is not your forte, It's secondary to your neck, Nectarine!

Giraffe: That's it: Do you have to?

Adam: You can't be called Do You Have To.

Eve: Dewey Half-twos. Half-Jew. Giraffe. How about giraffe?

Adam: Well, how about it? We haven't got all day, you know. I mean a day is now about 4% of all time on God's earth.

Eve: Whose, honey?

Adam: God's, silly. Don't tell me you haven't heard.

Giraffe: Ok. Giraffe is ok with me. I wanted to be Marilyn, but I'll accept giraffe. And by the way, we've been here a lot longer than a couple of weeks. Why I know my great grandmother. So you don't have to buy that God made the earth in seven days. It's what you want that you think is.

Eve: I know I should think something, but I'm just not sure what, so I don't.

Adam: Next.

Skunk: I'm nothing, you're nothing, and nothing makes sense except supping, sleeping, and shagging, with an occasional foray into the higher arts, of course.

Adam: Of course.

Skunk: And besides, no one gets near enough to me to call me by name anyway.

Adam: I think then you're a Faraway.

Skunk: Why don't you call me a Stink? You are so literal. What's in a name but my image? And besides, whatever you call me, I'll try to call myself something else.

Adam: As a citizen of the Garden, I'll let you call yourself whatever you want at home. But in the body politic you have to have a name to distinguish you from the others.

Skunk: Private Smelly Skunk, serial number 1234567, sir.

Adam: A citizen has responsibilities. But this ain't the army, brother.

Dodo: I won't even participate in this charade. I will not have my identity condensed into a name. I shall go forever nameless.

Adam: Then thou shalt not go much longer. No name, no consideration.

Dodo: This is just another way to control me. You want to have my name so you can tell me to do things. Once you name me I have lost half my self-determination. The whole idea of freedom is based on being able to change oneself as one changes a coat, a new one for each season.

Adam: And then you'll be harvested once and for all.

Dodo: So if I don't consent to have a name, you threaten me with death. Are you the executioner we've been hearing so much about?

Adam: I'm not threatening anything. I'm just telling you like it is. If you don't have and use your name, I can't call you to receive the blessings of the Garden.

Dodo: I did just fine until you came along.

Adam: I think I'll call you Thank You.

Dodo: You're welcome.

Adam: No, your name is Thank You.

Dodo: Reminds me of my cousin, Last First. Just couldn't fit the form.

Adam: I'm trying to say what I mean and you keep twisting it around.

Dodo: And your coercive naming principle is not twisted? Please.

Adam: You're just a don't do.

Snake: Not bad, Don't-do.

Dodo: I do so.

Adam: Then you're a doo-doo.

Dodo: Don't say doo-doo, say Do-Do.

Adam: And you're a snake.

Snake: Whatever you say, sir.
Adam: Now that's more like it. See, why can't you be more like him?
Dodo: Because I'm more like you.
Adam: What do you mean?
Dodo: You believe in progress, don't you?
Adam: Of course, it's getting better all the time.
Dodo: And you let that snake in the grass coddle up to you while you argue with other warm bloods.
Adam: I thought we were all one here in God's neighborhood.
Dodo: We are not. There is a definite hierarchy, and some claim a reason for the hierarchy. That's why we'e all afraid of you.
Adam: What do you mean?
Dodo: To be and not to be. That is reality. Whether it is nobler in the mind is not the question. Can you admit it varies?
Adam: I'm lost.
Dodo: We are all lost. The question is whether we should make up arrows pointing nowhere to reassure ourselves or can we admit uncertainty is our condition. No guarantees of being good enough to survive. Just survive as well as you try. No threatening life insurance, no organized reassurance. I am pure and I remain pure and nameless.
Adam: You too. You're a Dodo...or a Sergio Leone fan.
Dodo: Watch it, bud. I happen to have a perfect attitude.
Adam: Time's up. Now, sweeties, what I'd like to do here is run that through one more time for real, for the big boys.
Skunk: Just what I always wanted, an audience. (Enter angels)
Gabriel: Our lord your God has ordained that we be treated to the naming of the animals.
Adam: I live to serve your lordships and my words shall be my name.
Gabriel: Let the procession begin.
Adam: A wooly lamb precedes this Sheep into the world.
Sheep: I'm here for the sheer pleasure of it.
Gabriel: We see the beauty of your name and your person. You are a hallowed presence in our Garden and presage the coming of our lord and his followers to earth.
Adam: To prune the highest trees our Giraffe will ecologize.
Giraffe: I rise to the theme of the impending crisis of faith

that our Adam staunches.

Gabriel: Faith is renewed by his great works and by the sense of relief we feel. We understand that it needs renewal like the trees who lose their leaves.

Adam: And beyond the pale our Skunk wanders like a flower who lost his roots.

Skunk: It's not me that smells so bad, it's you who are smelling it. To me protection is divine.

Gabriel: You have such a wonderful smell. Would evolution have made such a hell?

Adam: The Dodo will not do what he is supposed to do and so he will be out-done
in time of which we know the outcome.

Dodo: I have said it once, and I've said it twice. This guy Adam is not treating me nice. I want to put in a formal complaint against this guy who says what he ain't. You are all making a pitch for God. To me it seems a trifle odd that I should believe what such as you say, who are all in the Big Guy's pay.

Gabriel: Oh, ye of little faith or brain. To speak so in his Garden is a little vain. But only time can heal the wound. I fear you don't know just how soon your time is going to be unturned.

Dodo: I will fight with my dying breath to end the injustice of being named.

Adam: And finally, your loving Snake who does what should be done when told.

Snake: I beseech thee to tread on your humble snake.

Gabriel: Quite a performance, Snake, but we remember you.

Snake: If you doubt my sincerity, put me to the test.

Gabriel: Since we are concerned to preserve the Garden, I would make you supporter of Adam in his role as resource manager, since this is why we have started the naming convention.

Skunk: I don't see too many Shriners around here.

Adam: Ask not what your Garden can do for you but what the God did for me when I was in Egypt.

Gabriel: Please, no hucksterism in the sight of God.

Dodo: Isn't that an oxymoron?

Adam: You've had your say.

Gabriel: I don't like the way this is progressing.

Adam: Depends on your model. If your goal is Armageddon, you can get it by positing a single point of origin. If your goal is advancing the cause of life on earth, you can get it too. The problem is stating the policy of multiplicity.

Gabriel: We must get back to our silver-lined cloud. These issues are too earthly.

Adam: We will remember you as you are here with us. (Exit Gabriel and angels)

Skunk: Now that you have categorized us, what shall we do? Fall to fighting among ourselves, no doubt.

Giraffe: I like knowing who I am.

Skunk: It's not who you are; it's what Adam says you are.

Sheep: Don't be so negative all the time. It makes my fleece shrink.

Skunk: I'm telling you what I think, not what you think. That's the difference between Adam and the rest of us. He's trying to set an agenda by his name game.

Dodo: I still refuse to be considered to have been named.

Skunk: That's quite a tense situation you've got there, sir. Or is it ma'am?

Giraffe: We giraffes don't have to talk to such riffraff.

Adam: And so you will not talk. (Exit Adam)

Snake: Well, I haven't offended anyone. You can talk to me.

Giraffe: (Points and gestures)

Dodo: See, it's started. She can't get a word in edgewise or any otherwise wise. I told you this would end badly.

Sheep: You are the bad end, Don't Do. If everyone had gone along with Adam, we wouldn't be in this fix.

Snake: I am getting an idea.

Skunk: Don't have a cow.

Snake: A snake can't have a cow any more than a chicken can have an egg.

Scene 5: Adam Downsizes Eden

Adam: I think the animals have too much freedom and are beginning to not appreciate all that we've done for them.

Eve: You mean productivity is down and waste is up; borrowing is rife and savings are drained; they are using too many resources and not replenishing the environment; they harbor ill-feelings and act in an anti-social manner while accepting the largess of the public weal; they are screwing around with the divine order you have established and not mentioning your name often enough in their scripts; they are heightening the blubber while not accommodating the gizmos on which we depend for evaluation; they mean nature in one scene and the masses in another and you're not in control of which; they market their homegrown and ask for foreign aid; they want more pay for less work; they want the profit while you take all the risks? You mean to say they take take take? Can you believe it?

Adam: I couldn't have said it myself.

Eve: Of course you can say it.

Adam: All right, it.

Adam decides that he should move the animals to the other side of the Eden border so that they can be made to work harder to get their food. Eve suggests they use the snake to woo the other animals to the border, while offering them not just the safe little world of Eden but a big world of opportunity and freedom.

Scene 6: Shift of Fools

Snake: I couldn't agree more.
Of course.
I concur
I absolutely think you're right about that
Certainly
You have hit the nail on the head
Right
That's right
While everybody else was going the wrong way, you were already staking your claim to reality.

There aren't many people who knew what to do in those days
Uh, huh.
Sure is.
Right
Correctamiento
Exactamiento
Precisely what I would have done
That shoe is on the right foot
Fits like a glove, I'd say
I sure would
Yes, yes, yes.
I couldn't disagree with that one.

Scene 7: The Garden

Sheep talking about her vulnerability as a sex object in a different character than she portrays as a sheep, perhaps a hardened Lower East Side actress.

Scene 8: Crossover

Adam: How did we get over?
Eve: I didn't know we were sick.
Adam: Feels like some kind of sick. Struggle and longing. I've had enough.
Eve: It's only been five minutes since we crossed.
Adam: More like eternity.
Eve: No, that's where we're going to burn for that fruit.
Adam: What a ghastly thought. Fried for a fruit.
Eve: Maybe it means something else.
Adam: Like what?
Eve: He's testing our resolve. He wants to see if we are still faithful to him after our punishment. Maybe if we stay faithful to him we'll be reinstated.
Adam: How do you know we've been exiled?
Eve: Gabriel left little room for doubt.
Adam: And the snake. I feel guilty about the snake.
Eve: Worry about yourself, Adam. You've got a lot to do.

Adam: Can we go back?
Eve: Back into the space where it was, but it's not there now.
Not for us.

Scene : In Eden After the Apple

(Sounds somehow different)

Giraffe: Futsky, butsky, futsky.
Skunk: Bitsky, shitsky, whiskey.
Dodo: Sucksky, wucksky, sucksy.
Snake: Sssssssssssssss.
Adam: What are they talking about?
Eve: Sounds pornographic to me. Shall we try it?
Adam: Fuck ing shit suck.
Giraffe: Who let them back in?
Snake: I posted the memo the other day. Hereinafter the
aforementioned Adam and Eve shall without restriction be
allowed to move freely across the boundaries of Eden.
Any denizen of Eden who notices a change in the behavior
pattern of Adam and Eve shall keep their noticing of such
a change to themselves.
Sheep: Then you're in violation again, snakey-pooh.

Continues.

Entangled Bank

2012-2016

BEAUTIFUL POEMS FOR MY FRIENDS

For John Ashbery at 80:
Your poems are so beautiful
Like stars in the night sky
That have become so good
At burning brightly

For Mei-mei Berssenbrugge:
You are beautiful
Well-dressed and beautiful
And read your beautiful poems
Beautifully in a beautiful voice

For Stacy Szymaszek:
You are beautiful
Beautiful and tough
A rebus of beauty
Frankly replying with both parts

For Evelyn Reilly:
You are beautiful
And accurate but chary
Of beauty really
Contradictory though it is

For Bob Holman:
You are beautiful
Fugitive and beautiful
Your motion blurs the edges
Where did you go?

For Norman Fischer:
You are beautiful
Defeated by beauty
Butter on your head
Words in the bellies of moths

For Michael Gottlieb:
You are a beautifully dressed poet
In beautiful, carefully-matched colors
Like a beautiful, green sea turtle
Paddling through beautiful sharp coral

For Ann Lauterbach:
You are so beautiful
When thunder cracks
And you jump beautifully
Coloring the page edge

For Nada Gordon:
You are beautiful
And you know it
It's funny too how you
Show it but that's alright

For Erica Kaufman:
You are beautiful
Generous and touch
To help and keep
All you know that's beautiful

For Drew Gardner:
You are beautiful
With surprising detail
In talk and music either
With surface to air missiles

For Kim Rosenfield:
You are beautiful
I caught you looking
Pitiless and forgiving
For thinking you beautiful

For Rob Fitterman:
You are beautiful
Hale and well met
And reworked several times
Without showing any cracks

For Gary Sullivan:
You are beautiful,
Spinning into the ether
Dancing on train roofs
On the string of a kite

For Bruce Andrews:
You are a beauty
A real beaut
Each syllable of beautiful
Has a beautiful, exploitable meaning all its own

For Charles Bernstein:
You are so afraid
To be beautiful except
That shy beauty that glam
Or else beautiful attitude

For Anne Waldman:
Your arms are beautiful
When you wave them
Over your beautiful head
Recalling us to mind.

For Me:
You are beautiful
Dutiful beautiful and
You write beautiful poetry
That everybody says, beautiful.

PASSIVE VOICE: FORCING AMARYLLIS

For the diarist in search of a life
The passive voice tastes good for my breakfast.
It somehow lends my work authority.
It rallies nobody's freedom but hope-flack,
That jumping spider, that achy-breaky
Crawl to middle ground
That implies,
As here,
Just how dear she was
To cling to who she was.

An EKG Addressed to Monody's Cloven Hoof
Forced change is climate's government
And with it the pretense of change.
Continuing to think it's only we,
It's only us,
A compromise constructs our towns
And brands defiant poet's voice.

While poverty pushes people passive,
Inequality drives us to the polls,
It's all we can do unless, unless
We're willing to risk a mess, a mess
As if risk itself assured success
Of our endeavors indeed.

While I'm deciding, women vivify
With figures of endurance,
Occasional resistance,
Ululating where the living mostly
Segment thought
And all the dead know is storytelling.

Citizens motivate through space,
Passive regarding fearsome time.

Thus, sweeter far than earthly strain,
Myselves be bling:
If you refuse to follow the spoor,
It's quite useless to force you.

Shall Pull Us to Glory Like Bricks
These lines voice submerged questions
Like "What?" and "How?" and "Where am I in this?"
Thus the voice of reason cries with winning force,
"wtf?" and "omg". Too often
The power of one organism fails
Even though addressed in the mail
And clung to when hearts sail.

Couching nature as bundles and linkages,
Channels and—you can't get more abstract from here—
Leap to march 'neath shriveling swords
To capture intuitions
Such as Bruce has been existing for a long time,
And Deborah is exactly what I would call a role model.

Science, that vast left-wing conspiracy
Aspiring, shifts from le lot quotidian
To moral force occurs in parts of a word—am, amar, rill,
An R construed as the whole highlights the limit
Of asserting, repeating, convincing no matter how loud,
Loud with all the facts
Our schooled and slangy children object
That the politics of resistance became a school for shoppers,

To Act With (Apparent) Centrifugal Force
Sparkling centrifuge, Persian miniatures
(meek. o'pasiv.o, voice calling
In the tangled debt (shard/shared
As spinning out rage,
As re-domesticating women after the revolution
Might be a task to resist)) spin.

My meter rounds off numbers,
To make sense shine in sharing.
For what can force or guile,
Their march loose from the rapid cars,
Do to save our world from us?

Long before The Origin of Species appeared
Evolution had been reconciling
Entangled thought with banks.
A person : an organism = an idea : a discipline = a poem :
an ecosystem.
Gone from a passive pursuit
To shouting, no longer a voice in the wilderness,
Agency and audience linked in devolution.

Font Dog Handbrake Virus!
This poem is dedicated to she
Whose spelling transformed measure.
As vigorous force and seeing words,
Cells make markets. Little Indians
Grabs their syllables to play.

Country tears in lyric bullets
Fall for my valentine's ringtones
While delusions of reference stream in retribution
For Bard, polemics, printer's ink.
Welcome to the Subscription Center and enhancement plan:
Tamales of Sparta rolled global.

Faceless Female Persona as Their "Other"
Everywhere you look these days
Funny pregnancy-cake wrestling decorations
Are disappointing women worldwide
While men insist big orgasm
Techniques're bustin' out
Cheat codes on Xbox realty.
Are these risky idioms networked
Into a single massive missive addressed to you?

Does novel poetry cheat happy sport street
Of a good time had by all?
How can I talk about someone else,
Except to accept others think otherwise?

Giving-no-quarter ignores
We're all in this together.
Art, as if to saddle a horse
With personal taste, be hers.
How do you account for neighbors?
Civil cases filed against low-protein piety?

Loose Coupling of Theory and Practice
Looking for poetry in all the wrong places,
Loose canons come with a good rhyme
And extended warranty, so
It's not easy to break those links
To the deeper inner you.

Speak, you poets.
Word up!
Smile at each other.
Negative capability doesn't mean bad attitude.

Loose coupling of theory and practice:
Loosely tied to spontaneous change,
Coupling through linkages like syntax;
Being is my connector.

What Did Lewis Carroll Do in Mathematics? Or John the Baptist Training Teaches You Not to Lose Your Head

1.
When interfering with power; don't glower.
Let your smile be your umbrella.
Undo their logic a capella.
"Three points are taken at random on an infinite plane.

Find the chance of their being
The vertices of an obtuse-angled triangle."
Alice Liddell's frame of probability, beyond what's plain,
Is the main chance when we're stuck
Listening to our gut where bacteria speak for us.

2.
What happens to your body when you release control
Of yourself, of your relations, of your views
To write words widely on purpose,
Not pinning pining hope to the page?
The angel on bended knee humanizes assembly.

Our prophetic mariner walking shoe
Exploits ethical validity
With the method trees use to estimate
And because your first step is often a long one.

3.
"If six cats can kill six rats in six minutes,
How many cats does it take to kill 100 rats in 50 minutes?"
Multiple solutions rule in Kevin Killian's coloring book.
Just how much thought is required to write a poem?
You think arbitrary is a problem? Arbitrary is a solution!
Look around you! We've recoupled.

Command-Operated Sheep Cruise aka Cardamom Spoofing
Large blooming amaryllis will have been forced.
The nature of humanity would have been mapped
By the Knicks Albanian hair removal faction, if not
By the Hindu clown penis, safe and alert for donors.
The kingdom of god suffers sore knees,
Tightly coupled. Then we're all set for a ride,
On a night train, teaching liar mechanics to undergrads,
Grievous Dream of Jeannie anti-glare windscreen coating,
And so I learn to write like Alan Davies?

Amaryllis nutrition
How to accept multiple solutions?
Same not yours to government health care
To diarrhea tractors
To feeding 9 billion amaryllis
Guantanamo amaryllis
Cheap, free, dual-channel, diesel-driven, nutrition-labeled, hackneyed, anti-theft, Ciceronian, amplified, framed, double, mobile, absolute, inevitable, ideal, long-stemmed amaryllis!

TRAINS ARTICULATION

(Please impute your own themes into this poem remembering what you don't know about it.)

It's conceivable
And appropriately seasonable,
Even if results
Aren't all that reasonable?

What's the weather
Between my fingers?
I dunno, ague?
Arguing, I'm sure; with Mondays.
Yeah, I knew, censure:
I don't remember anything about it.
They made me do it.
I was drunk.
Just following orders.

Suddenly it's quite quiet on the train
Except, of course, for breathing and tracks.
But the story gets longer.
I don't know whether clearer
But I'm saying you might want to hear her out.

Line me up with a corner.
Box me into come again.
I'm not and then feign,
Even if you claim
You are. Yet, I persist,
But don't want to wait.

A departure of the whole cell,
Actually, going against it,
Tonight. Not a planet at all
Going out with the light.

IN MEMORIAM

You will not care because you will not exist.
—Lucretius

No more memorial services for me
Where poets intone their own poems
Pretending to revere the dearly departed.
So here's the story:
My friends age, sicken and expire; what else to do?
Finally, I croak, too.
And none whose commemorative
I graced with my presence
Graces it with their presence.
The one I really care about I'll miss.

The Oligarch

2018

To the excellent Elon Musk:

Anyone who hopes to gain the favor of an oligarch offers what they think influential people enjoy. Supplicants present ostentatious building plans, brilliant patent filings, and expensive gifts such as cars, paintings, and baseball cards.

Although lacking the capital for such a princely offering, I am keen to bestow some proof of my appreciation. Thus, I present this treatise on the networks of power that I have written after years studying technology, finance, environment, and language.

These reflections, channeled through a work of great antiquity and importance, Niccolò Machiavelli's The Prince, remind us of the timeliness and timelessness of the subject of leadership by small groups. Some of the perspectives herein may contradict conventional wisdom, but I ask you to keep an open mind.

Though I consider this book barely worth your attention, I trust that you will be kind enough to accept it. The best gift I can offer is the opportunity to understand in the shortest time what I have learned through years of anguish and compromise, weathering the ubiquitous clamor and assault of disinformation.

Productive and effective people consider their relationships from many points of view and do not act on essential truths. Filmmakers photograph mountains from the plains, and in order to screen the plains, shoot from the peaks. There is no privileged position of comprehension. Diverse evidence must be correlated.

Take then, this little gift in the spirit that I offer it. If you consider it, it will become apparent how to reach the prominence promised by your skill, focus, and good fortune. And if, Elon, from your mountaintop, you sometimes turn your eyes to these lower regions, you will see how much your work means to the world.

Yours truly,
James Sherry

CHAPTER I: HOW MANY FORMS OF GOVERNANCE THERE ARE AND HOW THEY OPERATE

All states and all companies that rule and have ever ruled function and have functioned as oligarchies. While there are multiple forms of governance such as republics, principalities, and corporations, all operate through control by a few.

Oligarchies are transmitted either by tradition, inheritance, or law, or they are new. In most cases, they are organized by agreement about principles and based on individual merit, but sometimes oligarchic power is inherited. New oligarchies are either entirely new, as the United States of America was for Alexander Hamilton, Thomas Jefferson, and James Madison, or they are created from established states and companies, as in the case of the European Union, pillared on trade and banking.

Some oligarchies operate through the illusions of autocratic form as in Russia, where President Vladimir Putin's prominence conceals the cadre of oligarchs that runs the state and the economy. Other oligarchies live with the delusions of democracy as in the US, where the people have little control over their economic, political, and cultural fate, yet they insist they are free. In Russia, oligarchs use the autocracy to control and sequester financial and hard assets. In the US, oligarchs establish freedom of action for themselves to accumulate assets and control institutional processes. Freedom for the people means something quite different, as you well know.

Oligarchies in modern times are acquired either through the arms of defense industries, as in Europe after World War II; by the manipulation of popular uprisings, as with China and the Soviet Union; or by a supportive external oligarchy, as in Chile via the US-backed assassination of Salvador Allende, or in Iraq via the toppling of Saddam Hussein.

The forms of governance have received the detailed attention of political writers from Plato and Aristotle to Machiavelli and Montesquieu to Karl Marx and Thorstein Veblen, as well as through the theory of corporations, the media, and contemporary political cant. Operations, on the other hand, are obscured by immense detail and secrecy. These operational details, as much as form, regulate individual well-being. Operational skills determine individual and group successes. How political leaders operate within the form of government determines their ability to hold office and avoid unnecessary conflict. How corporate leaders operate a firm determines its profitability.

Rather than provoke a conflict in defense of form, which we all value, this book focuses on the networks of leadership that link form and operations. The driving forces behind visible leaders are these oligarchic networks that support presidents and CEOs in top administrative positions. Leadership is layered and not based on that cult of individuals that culture promotes. Gaining support from the people requires formal consent and general consensus. Consent of the governed has been accomplished in modern times by broadening suffrage, increasing representation in government, and disseminating effective public relations. State and corporate public relations identify coalitions whose supporters are often asked to act in a manner contrary to their self-interest. The Enlightenment ideals of freedom of the mind and action have captured the support of both the masses and the intelligentsia. But state and corporate mechanisms of control have increasingly invalidated these freedoms through operational changes that override the will of the majority of citizens and workers, allowing oligarchs to increase their share of wealth and power.

Truly, democracy usually improves the well-being of the people. Yet too little consideration has been given to how different forms of governance actually function and who benefits. And it is on the other side of this scrim of form that power is wielded throughout the world.

CHAPTER II: CONCERNING OLIGARCHIES TRANSMITTED BY TRADITION, INHERITANCE, OR LAW

Republics, autocracies, and public and private companies operate similarly through control by small groups, the differences being their form, public face, and how surplus is distributed. Form alone does not determine the value of a state or corporation. Democracies impoverish their people nearly as often as autocratic forms of government and do not guarantee individual happiness and security. Zimbabwe, Haiti, and India are examples of different governmental forms of notably inequitable states in which large swaths of people suffer unnecessarily due to the uneven distribution of wealth and self-serving leadership. Singapore and Germany have healthy, productive populations in spite of differing forms.

Although the personal freedom promised by democracy usually improves individual well-being, a state government must balance economic conditions with appropriate taxation and benefits to reduce suffering and precarity among its citizens. Equality of opportunity and balancing wealth improve any organization more than too few receiving too much of either. Lower net inequality is robustly correlated with faster and more durable growth, for a given level of redistribution. If politicians and economists do not cleave too tightly to the interests of any one class, they well understand the tipping points of economic equality, after which political instability increases.

Economic power is one of the chief supports of any oligarch. You need money to pursue your programs. But the media phrase "follow the money," like vulgar Marxism, misdirects the oligarch's understanding of power by proposing a single, essential criterion for control. It creates factions among citizens and intensifies the desire for personal wealth. Looking more closely, other types of control, influence, and organization sustain power's infrastructure. Including elites—and not just the wealthy—in understanding how the few rules promotes greater accuracy about power, since the leadership network and the character of its connections, as much as wealthy individuals, shape any organization. This network continually transmits power and reroutes change throughout time and social structure, usually permitting one individual to easily replace another in leadership roles. Effective bureaucratic communications account for the longevity of certain states and cultures as much as other vectors like predictable water flows.

This network, like any complex system, operates similarly at different scales. Although the form of communications is specific to each organization, transmissions within a family or clan contain similar information to those of the corporation or state. Peace cannot be made between warring factions without go-betweens who are familiar with both sides of a dispute. Lawyers standardize methods and protect clients in commercial negotiations. Conflicts of interest are eliminated by rules developed by professional associations.

Protocols are often transformed when they pass from one entity to another or move between oligarchic groups. In Somaliland, for example, in 1999 businessmen stopped paying taxes to unreliable warlords, and transferred control of their commercial disputes to the Sharia courts of the Islamic Court Union. The ICU, made up of clan elders, businessmen, and sheikhs, derived its reliability from traditional connections to the powerful Hawiye clan of Mogadishu. This need for consistency in legal cases, especially contract law, drives oligarchs to standardize and reduce the likelihood of miscommunication. Co-location of private assets such as the endowment of the Basilica of St. Mark in Venice and offshore banking institutions such as those in the Cayman Islands and Switzerland exemplify such standards that assure oligarchs that assets are protected yet accessible to them.

The network holds sway over individuals, even the richest and strongest, and supports operations at all scales from local to global. The network's most powerful and stable nodes—both individuals and groups—tend to be those with the most connectors to other nodes, not only those with the most money or the biggest armies. Their connections are strong or weak, continuous or intermittent, mono- or bidirectional depending on conditions, but relative reliability remains vital to any channel. Hence financial transactions are matched at exchanges controlled by well-documented rules.

Highly connected individuals and groups build and defend corporations and states. Focusing only on wealthy individuals reinforces a marginal participant's desire to join these networks, acting as an incentive to join the bureaucracy. Such media focus fetishizes consumption and disguises the reins of power, since power that proclaims itself loses power. So, it is usually in the interests of an oligarch to work in the background, hence the effectiveness of oligarchs in democracies. The combined wealth and stability of civil oligarchs compares favorably to ruling oligarchs who, while potentially richer—compare the net worth of Russia's Putin to Microsoft's Bill Gates—operate at greater risk.

An oligarch finds fewer difficulties in managing states and corporations with traditional oligarchies. For example, in England, leadership was so secure it attracted much of the Venetian gold that fled its Republic prior to Napoleon's conquest in 1798. Newly minted wealth, as in Silicon Valley, is more troublesome because culture develops slowly within any domain. It takes a while for an oligarch to stabilize power relations, but it is usually sufficient to prudently address situations as they arise and avoid transgressing the customs of precursors. If a new leader like US President Jimmy Carter appears, whenever anything sinister happens to him, like an October surprise, another group ascends because culture is built around existing expectations.

The Koch brothers, Charles and David, could not have withstood the attacks of political foes if they had not been well established in the oil refineries they inherited from their father, Fred. Using that base, they sustainably diversified their holdings. They have networked conservatives for decades, building new organizations like the Cato Institute to project their power and installing their people in existing institutions like George Mason University through funding from their private foundations. They also fund the American Civil Liberties Union, prison reform efforts, and other moderate institutions that can promote aspects of libertarianism and provide suitable cover for their activities. Their network is not limited to any form of governance, but rather extends freedom of action for themselves.

The Koch brothers' notion of freedom implies that they benefit from democracy, although universal suffrage actually impedes their progress. As a result, Koch-funded organizations actively work to suppress voters in many jurisdictions. Along with other highly connected citizens like Karl Rove, lobbyist Jack Abramoff, Congressman Bob Ney, and billionaires Paul Singer and Julian Robertson, this network has, through the good offices of many Secretaries of State, like Florida's Katherine Harris and Kansas' Kris Kobach, wiped more than seven million legitimate registered voters from the rolls, mostly Democrats, students, the elderly, and people of color.

Hereditary and traditional oligarchs are unlikely to offend existing cultures. The people feel these multigenerational leaders act as they themselves have been taught to behave. In this way, all parties are apparently respected. Unless extraordinary behavior, like Howard Hughes', causes a hereditary oligarch to be mistrusted, the network will continue to support their control. Due to the duration of oligarchic hegemony, the memories and motives that drive change fade. In this way, the hereditary oligarch uses time to moderate social change.

Hereditary oligarchies, however, suffer from an inherent weakness: a scion may not have the same strength of mind or purpose as the fortune's founder. As a result, most developed nations have severely restricted the institutional guarantees of the power of inherited, aristocratic wealth. If the blood has thinned due to the chances of genetics or aesthetic training, leadership is often inherited by weaker hands. These children of oligarchs may let power slip from their grasp either by running the (e)state into the ground or by allowing it to be managed by professional administrators while they pursue their pleasure, good works, and art. If the former, then new, stronger hands will pick up the reins, and not much is lost.

But if the latter is the case, as often happens with inherited power and privilege, the (e)state is managed by lawyers and accountants—an industry that protects wealth—who have more interest in financial success than maintaining a socially responsible state or corporation. Even with the proper incentives, these professional administrators who preserve inherited wealth often promote unfair, even brutal, treatment of employees and citizens to assure profitability. The supported oligarchs, while rich beyond imagining, do not have the skills to maintain the integrity of the state or firm. The children of the Walton family appear as a fine example of disengaged, inherited wealth and power. Instead of enhancing Walmart's overall value, they allow it to be run in a way that ignores, as much as feasible, the society and infrastructure that made their wealth possible. In such cases, imbalances and inequality may become intolerable. Then the oligarchy itself becomes as vulnerable as France was in 1789 and Russia and China were in the twentieth century. Today, rising inequality, in developed countries such as the US and United Kingdom and in developing countries such as Russia and China, has begun to create imbalances and divergences—economic, political, and environmental—that suggest a turning point for humanity and a potential return of aristocratic institutional rights and privileges.

We cannot build a productive society, as highly interdependent and connected as our current world, by empowering the scions of hedge-fund managers and technology geeks. Inherited wealth can be effectively moderated by taxation, even against the efforts of the accountants and lawyers of the income protection industry. Recent studies have concluded that the equitable distribution of income is more important contributor to sustained economic growth than openness to trade, a competitive exchange rate, level of foreign investment, or the quality and stability of a country's political institutions. Taxing inherited wealth is in the interests of all but the feckless inheritors and the hollow arguments of paternalists.

Although the US separated from Europe to avoid aristocracy, the dynamics of both society and biology make limiting dynastic aspirations difficult. Thwarting the reproduction of strong lineage remains contrary to important inherent processes, since people constantly seek to perpetuate their names and genes through their children. Even non-human interactions in animal and plant kingdoms benefit from strong individuals. Yet farsighted leaders, such as Gates and Warren Buffet, turn over the majority of their assets to the public good, while making sure their children are comfortable and encouraging them to be active. Such strategies create more stable and widely supported societies.

The people, by virtue of their numbers alone, moral considerations aside, must participate in the economies of any state for it to succeed. In China, the Qing empire, isolated from its people, allowed its economy to stagnate and fall early in the twentieth century. The impoverished populace was unable to continue to support the state. A new stable oligarchy did not arise until 1949. It remains in power today, although incursions from financialized Western influence have increased inequality in China.

When too much wealth collects in the top strata, society stagnates and the environment suffers. When society stops channeling wealth to the bottom 90 percent, who spend earnings with a 3.6 times multiplier in the economy, but instead deliver tax breaks to the top 0.1 percent, whose multiplier is fractional, it should come as no surprise that organizations fail to thrive. Then the wise oligarch must take responsibility for rebalancing rather than increasing inequality.

Financial inequality is currently increasing in civil oligarchies like the US and EU, where the people lack sufficient income to buy enough of the products that enrich oligarchs to maintain vibrant economic growth. Instead, the people become disaffected from the lack of prospects and look beyond existing networks to recapture the wealth and control they imagine they had or should have. Further isolated by unsupportive corporate cultures within identity groups, populations exhibit extreme beliefs and behaviors as in the US elections of 2016 and the Brexit vote in the UK. Recognition of this debilitating social situation by a far-sighted oligarch and well-connected groups might help stabilize and turn around societies at risk of collapse from wealth inequality and climate change driven by the oligarchs' desire for ever-greater power, wealth, and the false sense of security they offer.

CHAPTER XV: CONCERNING THINGS FOR WHICH ALL PEOPLE, AND ESPECIALLY OLIGARCHS, ARE PRAISED OR BLAMED

What ought to be the rules of conduct for an oligarch towards citizens, employees, and peers? Since many have written on this point, you may consider it presumptuous to mention it again, especially because we are taking a different point of view than the authorities. Nevertheless, to write something useful for you who wish to understand and not simply confirm what you already believe, it appears more appropriate to identify the complexity of these matters than to decorate a generality that stirs our emotions.

Many have idealized the form of government—Aristotle, Hobbes, Jefferson, Marx, Chomsky—describing republics and principalities that never existed. Many have tried to establish a single set of principles for right action. But because humanity cannot be fully represented alone and separate from the rest of the planet, these writer's prior principles remain divorced from the detailed interactions that take place between the layers of political, ethical, and environmental conditions daily played out on many stages. Prioritizing any one discipline, like economics, ethics, and self-interest, under all conditions, however reassuring, cannot be the basis of an oligarch's policies. What's good for the goose is sometimes not good for the glance.

The thorough application of any single principle sooner results in an oligarch's ruin than your preservation. If you wish to live up to your public professions of virtue, you must recognize that important actions often have some elements of uprightness and some of injustice. The oligarch benefits from separating, for example, investments for social utility and investments for personal profit. Mixing these two, while profitable in the short term, leaves a bitter taste in the mouths of your citizens and workers. It sets a bad example for the public and for other leaders. Focusing solely on the idea of your freedom, without understanding how the exercise of freedom may turn out to be no more than license. And if you ignore fairness and equality, or at least the appearance of them, you expose your regime to internal dissent. An oligarch's fortunes and humanity are reinforced by recognizing the multiple, often contradictory, effects of your actions.

Both oligarchs and planners in oligarchic networks must know how to apply the principles outlined above to balance the multiple effects of their actions and to use them to retain and improve their position. Putting on one side the myths concerning oligarchy, like conspiracy theories, and discussing on the other those acts which are material, all people exhibit qualities which bring them both blame and praise. One is reputed liberal, others miserly. One is reputed generous, one rapacious; one cruel, one compassionate; one faithless, another faithful; one cowardly, another bold and brave; one affable, another arrogant; one lascivious, another chaste; one sincere, another cunning; one hard, another easy; one grave, another frivolous; one religious, another unbelieving; one racist, another less prejudiced; and the like. These characteristics follow the oligarch around, and the media tend to report news items that reinforce these binaries in order to sell papers and capture eyeballs.

Everyone wishes an oligarch to exhibit only the good qualities named above. Such consistent behavior isn't always possible in the public arena or in private business. Because an oligarch's motives and thoughts can't be traced through every complex transaction, it is only necessary to be sufficiently careful to avoid those vices which would lose you your position.

In the run-up to the 2016 US presidential election, FBI Director James Comey acted in a way that both affected the outcome of the election and remains opaque regarding his intention. Within a few days of exonerating Hillary Clinton of any legal wrongdoing with respect to her use of a private email account as secretary of state, Comey announced that the FBI had new information and might open a new inquiry concerning Clinton's emails. His action was significant in changing public opinion regarding Clinton's candidacy. Then once Trump had, with Comey's assistance, won the presidency, Comey refuted Trump's claim that prior President Obama had tapped his phones and began an investigation into Trump's ties with Russia. Trump's response was to fire Comey, claiming he did so because of Comey's self-serving behavior in speaking about Hillary Clintons emails, but Comey had stopped publicly discussing ongoing FBI investigations of Trump's business dealings, Russian influence, and cases against Trump for sexual misconduct.

It's easy to say that Comey was simply doing his job, serving the cause of justice and upholding the reputation of the FBI for unimpeachable honesty. It is also, however, relevant to say that he created a definitive power base for himself, announcing quite publicly that no one could gain or keep high office without including him and his bureau in the inner circle of decision-making. Hence, the details of such transactions are often opaque or ambiguous. To understand power, therefore, we must look at the outcomes of events to determine their significance and not waste time with unstated motives, praise, and blame because analysis of political systems is not a court of law, but only a way to clarify the ecology of events.

An oligarch should, when possible, avoid those associates who would hurt your reputation. But since, too, this is not always possible, you can employ problematic associates when appropriate, and use public relations to manage opinion with a combination of public press and social media. Colonial powers like the UK and

US often find local tyrants like Hosni Mubarak and Saddam Hussein useful in managing their foreign holdings. You don't need to make yourself uncomfortable by incurring blame for those vices without which the state and corporation could only be saved with difficulty. An occasional foray into the territory of a weaker state may do more to improve your popularity with the voters than it hurts you for appearing to bully weaker nations. Neither Reagan's attack on Granada nor Il Duce's on Ethiopia reduced their effectiveness as leaders. For, if considered carefully, something that looks like virtue, if followed, would be ruinous, while something else, which looks like vice, brings you security and prosperity.

An experienced oligarch knows what will bring you praise and blame as well as what blame will hobble your ability to act in the future. As mentioned, political and corporate management focus on outcomes more than ethics. This is not to say that the ends justify the means, but rather that intention doesn't always produce predictable results. Futilely searching for primary cause or ethical intention in complex situations is often nothing more than validating the searcher's self-image.

While trust remains a key component in the success of any activity, it is important to understand that associates can be trusted in some matters but not in others. Not coincidentally, contemporary medical best practices also focus on outcomes as a way to keep costs low and patients healthy over the entire system of medical care. Excellence in caring for the sick includes both quality services and assurance of good outcomes. In other multidisciplinary activities like war and electoral politics, individual actions can only be counted successful if outcomes also are successful. Both short- and long-term results must be documented in order to assess outcomes and which tactics that appear risky may often save the day. An oligarch is better served by attending to the longer term, as long as short-term reversals do not disrupt networks and risk losing one's position. Sometimes, however, you must be willing to lose a battle if the battle is only a distraction in the larger scheme of the war. Strategic sacrifice helps ensure longer term goals.

This point certainly does not suggest ignoring the details of transactions. In contemporary electoral politics, focusing on each vote and each category of votes in all jurisdictions determines how oligarchs are viewed by citizens and importantly whether they will win an election. Suppressing the votes of blacks, Hispanics, the elderly, the poor, and students in as many strategic jurisdictions in the US as possible determined Republican control of Congress in 2014 and Trump's victory in the presidential election of 2016 even though he received a minority of votes.

The US Constitution, through the Electoral College, is structured to balance the interests of the states with those of the nation. With increasingly large populations in only a few states, the less populated states have more control than a purer democracy would predict. Thus, practical electoral politics in the US and in other federal systems are successful when controlled by a few local oligarchs who are focused on the operations required to get friendly voters to the polls while suppressing opposition voters rather than focusing on the form of democracy. Electoral practices—purging voter rolls, caging votes by not forwarding registration forms to new addresses, spoiling votes as in the decision on hanging chads in Florida in 2000, blocking people from voting, stuffing ballot boxes, and crosschecking and then purging similar names suppressed in other states—are practical ways of reducing the other party's votes without much chance of being exposed in the media, except in the most superficial way.

Media in the US have little interest in actively questioning the electoral process, even when political parties engage in illegal practices. Media outlets would prefer to provide balanced reporting that avoids incurring the wrath of either side of a dispute and to establish false equivalences that make it difficult to assign blame to either side. Since Karl Rove and other electoral specialists have determined how to control voting out of the public eye, democracy as a form of government appears increasingly ineffective. This weakening of democratic franchise hastens the fall of US power around the globe. Tactical operations establish the order of oligarchy even as an oligarch is advised to maintain a longer view.

Oligarchs are vulnerable when they make complex decisions in the public view. Concern for sustainability and the common good are better drivers of action than morals. Although morals cannot lead oligarchic decisions, public outrage can imperil an office, and the pangs of conscience drain your resolve. Ethical evaluations, framed in a utilitarian manner as fulfilling the potential of a given situation while causing the least harm, may cause bad press and need spinning for different audiences such as Twitter and Foreign Affairs magazine. And sometimes such utility spirals out of control in public fora. Hence, balancing contradictory forces and opinions remains the most important skill in governing yourself and others. If your individual capacity for balance fails, you will be brought down by your enemies, although usually, as we have noted, it takes more than one fault to destroy a strong oligarch well positioned in the network.

CHAPTER XXVI: AN EXHORTATION TO LIBERATE NATIONS AND THEIR CITIZENS FROM MARKETPLACE MENTALITY

We have considered the ecosystems of politics. We have wondered whether present times are favorable for a new leader to emerge who acknowledges the interdependence of networks and the value of cooperation. We have weighed whether current conditions might present an opportunity for far-sighted oligarchs to introduce an order based on mutual aid. Such an order would honor them individually and collectively, improving the wellbeing of the people as well as helping to stabilize politics and the biosphere. It appears that so many things favor such changes that there is no time like the present to act.

The current situation seems ideal for creating an alternative to the competitive financialization of so many human activities that should be freed from the marketplace mentality such as education, delivery of medical care, elections, legislating, and economic opportunity. Institutions in the developed world have been debased by finance, fetishizing human relations and corrupting our environment. A new generation of oligarchs can now make apparent how the current situation may be changed and the people liberated from the appetites of finance. It may also turn out that financial matters themselves will benefit from being applied in appropriate situations, rather than treating every interaction as commercial.

Such a spark has been shown by one oligarch, who makes us think that he intends to support our survival as a species by creating technologies for broad use that do not further degrade the biosphere. We hope that other oligarchs will not reject him entirely in spite of their differing values. We hope they will not regress behind a wall of short-term self-interest, although stress tends to drive short-term behaviors. Instead, world leaders might use their networks to support the direction of this new oligarch, since it is to the majority's benefit in the long run to replace fossil fuels and eschew the marketplace model in those activities listed above. The majority of the people worldwide are ready and willing to follow this banner, if he will raise it in conjunction with others of like mind, so that thoughtful and powerful people everywhere can pursue sustainable policies, invention, and productivity.

We do not now see any others in whom we can place more optimism. Your illustrious endeavors with their forward-looking investments, your awareness of the interactions of the many components of indigenous life, and your willingness to be as transparent as possible with the people about opportunities for human improvement reduce how much our activities compromise the integrity of our surroundings. Such advances will be aided by recalling the actions and lives of the leaders we have discussed. Although they were great, they were human, and none of them had more opportunity than the present offers. Their situation was not more supportive of them than yours of you.

Those of us—activists, intellectuals, artists, and organizers—working for change seek environmental justice, recognizing the imbalances in society, as well as the biosphere. Change is happening all the time and is accelerating in recent years. If we don't change ourselves, we become victims of change instead of benefiting from it or at least accommodating our cultures to it. As with this book, we take the best of what is given, common, well-considered, and constant in our surroundings and, while maintaining its value, add what is changing to improve our understanding and to benefit the majority as well as creating opportunity for adventurous individuals. This book has hardly needed to invent and invents throughout. This recycling strategy combines with this book's subject matter, to illustrate how both specialized and interdisciplinary knowledge support our lives.

Many progressive endeavors have failed. Financial interests labor to make it appear that the marketplace, if left to itself, would be more propitious than regulatory intervention. But in fact, markets are inherently regulated and well organized. The market stalls are arranged in aisles. They may be regulated by participants for their own benefit, as in the oxymoronic free market, or they may be regulated by a combination of market participants and governments seeking to benefit the people, as well as the primary participants. These latter are the most successful marketplaces. Even a cursory look at past financial cycles supports this perspective. When regulation that accommodates both the needs of the people and leading market participants is withdrawn, mistakes are costlier, and private losses are charged to the public treasury. This occurs because ultimately the markets are a reflection of and in some cases a driver of economies. The arcane contention that the markets are always right is true only after the fact and does not imply that markets should lead policy, because markets are unpredictable. The logical fallacy, post hoc ergo propter hoc, applies to this argument. Finally, well-regulated markets increase demand, since low demand remains the key problem in highly unequal economies. Even if government regulation makes errors, those errors are not as costly to the society as those errors foisted on the people by leading market participants playing a winner-take-all game.

If too many parts of society operate on a marketplace model, even those that are actually active markets will not benefit because the other parts of the economy will drag them down too. We have seen this suppressed growth and financial repression in developed nation economies since the great recession of 2007. Components such as education and health care suffer because education is not about discovering the price for a degree, but about enhancing the benefits to students. Medical care seeks to improve the health and well-being of patients and to prevent illness, rather than to maximize the profit of antibiotics or surgery.

In addition, healthy people contribute to society and thereby benefit the largest number of people, including pharmaceutical executives.

When marketplace mentality is applied to education, university boards comprised of developers benefit from building projects, but students suffer from higher costs, scholastic standardization, and less attention paid to their education. When the marketplace model is applied to medicine, the health of the people suffers so that in the US, where the market dominates medical practice, lifespans are shorter, infant mortality is higher, productivity suffers from poor nutrition, and the increase in medical technology for the few is not significantly better than in countries where all citizens' health is paid for by a single-payer system, and the market, while not ignored, isn't primary.

In a marketplace of political candidates where oligarchs throw billions at legislators to control them, the people no longer support the government and think government is the problem. The people think it is government's fault that governance is arrogant. In actuality, misdirected oligarchs both in and out of government fail to understand their long-term self-interest and only consider getting laws passed to benefit their bottom line. This is true in the courts and the executive as well as in the legislatures, since all three branches of US government must now pay for their offices and cannot spend time on the people's business. The body politic falls ill and suffers when leaders operate mainly to benefit their factions.

The opportunity, therefore, should not be allowed to pass to let the media at last see leaders appear who can help the world rebalance. You cannot underestimate the support that you would receive in all those jurisdictions that have suffered from financialization and high-level corruption. What door would remain closed? And of course, you will remain modest in your demands.

Who would refuse to support clean transportation and energy at competitive prices, since energy must be cost effective for all to thrive? What resentment, besides certain vested interests that we have carefully noted, would inhibit progress, when not only the biosphere would benefit, but also when an environmental model of society prioritizes balance?

Such a model would encourage each component of our society to manifest itself both on its own terms and together. This model of diversity implies that all components will not thrive under the same criteria, since each has unique features that make it vital for medicine to be managed medically, education educationally, and politics politically rather than treating all human interactions as driven by a marketplace abstraction.

Let, therefore, your illustrious firms take up this charge with such courage and hope as all just enterprises are undertaken, so that under its standard our world may be moved back from the brink. And under your auspices may be realized that saying of Wordsworth:

> *Come forth into the light of things,*
> *Let Nature be your Teacher.*

The Rapture

2019

Produced by Inter Poets Theater
in association with Artists Space
Performed on Zoom Web
Sunday, December 6, 2020, 7:30pm EST

Act 1 Scene 1
Act 1 Scene 2
Act 1 Scene 4
Act 2 Scene 3
Act 3 Scene 4
Act 4 Scene 4
Epilogue

Act 1, Scene 1: CEO and Minister discuss increased human population

(Image projection of Dubai or WTC, might consider old twin towers to emphasize the impact)
Two characters: CEO (1) & Minister (2)

CEO:
Our new drug, Longeva,
is saving millions of lives.
Minister: But our funeral parlor division,
I mean, brethren,
are having a bad year.
And frankly, the lord receives
fewer funeral prayers.
My intention is not to offend,
but that drug of yours, sir,
turned my flock into zombies.
CEO: Longeva drives more
revenue than your losses.
Even with the miniscule percentage
of zombie side effect—
and no double-blind test proved that effect.
The purpose of civilization is
to keep people alive, healthy,
and most of all productive?

Minister:
Yes, I guess. I mean, of course.
But god's planet suffers
under the weight of so many people.
There are 50% more people on Earth
than it can sustainably support.

CEO:
Are you talking climate change,
that junk science?

Minister:
My sermon Sunday addresses available resources.
We have limited arable land.
Water supplies are dwindling.
With this population we'll use up
potable water everywhere.
Seas are rising and your firm
wants to save millions more lives.
God needs those souls.

CEO:
Technology's the solution, preacher.
We can go to Mars.
Think of the profits.

Minister:
There is another factor here.

CEO:
What's that?

Minister:
My prayers to heaven have been answered.
God wishes increases in human mortality.
He's got idle angels lolling about
restless. He fears instability.
The supply chain is underutilized.
Angels not processing enough souls
to gain their bonus level wings.
In terms that you would use, sir,
lower death rate means
lower profits from Earth
and excess capacity in heaven.
The soul supply needs a shock.
God and Jesus think
it's time for Jesus to come again.

CEO:

WHAT?
Minister:
The Rapture first
then the Second Coming.
The Lord is my shepherd.

end scene

Act 1 Scene 2: Mother & Student-Daughter fight in the dining room

(Image of split-level tract home)
Two characters: Student-Daughter (6) & Mother (5)

Student-Daughter:
I'm home, Mom.
Chose my major today.
A finance degree it is!
About time someone around here
made some money. If the world had more
women running businesses,
then businesses would be better.

Mother: (startled)
Wait a minute! Just a few weeks ago,
we were talking about Women's Studies
or Environmental Studies. Fields where
you can do some good work.

Student-Daughter:
That was a whole month ago.
I got some good advice
from my school counsellor
on where the action really is.

Mother:
Do you understand what you're saying?
Don't you know what it means to work
for a big corporation? Greedy people

who make a living taking the money
from hard, honest working folks.

Student-Daughter: (laughs) Pretty old-fashioned way
of looking at it, Mom. Corporations
do all sorts of environmental work.
Wearing flowers in your hair
is so 20th century.

Mother:
I was never a hippie,
I was a punk. I had a nose ring.
For two years I even had a mohawk.

Student-Daughter:
Hippie, punk, whatever.
I'm sure you looked very vintage
but I'm the one
who has to payback these loans.

Mother:
I promised I would help you.

Student-Daughter:
On your salary?
I don't really believe that,
and I don't want help
you can't afford. I certainly don't want
Dad's help either. If I never speak
to him again, that's fine with me.

Mother:
The corporate world made your Dad
who he is, a man loyal
to money and his pleasures.
And now you want to follow in his footsteps?

Student-Daughter:
I'm not following in his footsteps
or yours either. How do you know
that it won't be corporations who end up
saving the planet? They have all sorts of initiatives.
It's possible to make good money
and save the world.

Mother:
I don't want to argue.
I have an actual big fight coming up.
These Jesus freaks are really
making my life miserable.

Student-Daughter:
Don't they have a right
to be whoever they want to be?
Don't I have that right?

Mother:
They do, and you do,
but I think they're the ones
who want us to be just like them.
I'm happy to live and let live,
but I don't want to make a pilgrimage
to Jesus-a-Logo to genuflect
to the corporate shills in the pool.

Student-Daughter: (shakes head dismissively)
Maybe there's something in this Rapture
for me, for all of us. You've never even once
taken me to church. Maybe I want more
of a relationship with God.
Mother:
Honey, please don't be naive.
A lot of people start out
with the best intentions and end up

somewhere they never expected.
Student-Daughter:
Maybe I'll break the glass ceiling
instead of standing around
complaining about it. Things are different now, Mom.
It's possible to work inside the system. Me and my friends
are going to make the world the way we want it
to be. We're not like you;
we're not going to compromise.

Mother:
I thought you felt I was the one
refusing to compromise.

Student-Daughter:
Mom. You just don't get it, do you?
end scene

Act 1, Scene 4: Corporate leaders sell Tulsa to Russia

(Photo of signing of NAFTA or other treaty)
Four characters: CEO (1), Russian Oligarch (3), Mayor of Tulsa (4), Sergeant (6)

Mayor of Tulsa:
Jesus says, "Go, sell what you have."
Gentlemen, we folks weren't managing
our people and property effectively
here in Tulsa. Tax income was down 20%.
Home foreclosures up 8, crime up 10.
Democrats want social programs: too expensive.
Republicans lowered taxes on the upper brackets
and retail sales fell.
But this new opportunity
will make our town roar.
We should have leased you
Tulsa years ago.

CEO:
Tulsa needs a streamlined economy.
Cities can't be responsible
for too many poor citizens,
And the government of Tulsa
Consistently operates at a loss. Today's new
U.S./Russia "pilot program" leases cities
for 99 years to our northeastern neighbors.
You Russians know how to manage populations.
I'm sure you can reform the city
Without all those nasty human rights
That makes U.S. cities so expensive.

Russian Oligarch:
Mr. Mayor or I should call you
Grand Duke of the Greater Tulsa
of Russia, I'm so happy you've found
a vehicle to fit your new title.
I'm sure you'll help us run this city,
assuring all Tulsa citizens
Have—and know (he smiles)—their place.
We hear the work camps
are up and running, and that unemployment
is now practically zero.

Mayor:
We here in Tulsa are ready
for new trends:
Half corporate state, half work camp.
I'm sure we'll be squeezing
the best from everyone.

Russian Oligarch:
Mr. Mayor, of course.
Even the poorest citizens will have clear roles
with Tulsa in our hands.
Sergeant: (entering and saluting in the new way)
Mr. Mayor, the work camps are full.
We need more farmers to feed the workers.

Mayor: (frowns, annoyed)
Farmers? Yeah. Here in Oklahoma
we plowed them under in the Dust Bowl.
I hear some big farmers are going
To the big Jesus rally this weekend
down at Jesus-a-Logo.
Maybe we can talk to them there?

CEO:
A big bash, I hear. But I also hear
there's going to be a protest.

Oligarch:
Jesus saves us from worker complaints, poor people
And most activists. As long as he leaves
those lovely loopholes in his morality,
we can deal with a few meddlesome lefties.

CEO:
A few protestors reassure me
That I'm doing my job.

end scene

Act 2, Scene 3: Zombie congregation

(Image from Night of the Living Dead)
Three characters: First Zombie (2), Second Zombie (3), Third Zombie (6)
(Two zombies shake dirt off themselves)

First Zombie:
What a relief.
I feel great.
(moves around, exercising)

Second Zombie: Again? Have we been raised
from the dead again? I'm getting sick
of being raised from the dead.
We're shifted from death to insignificance

and inarticulate.
First Zombie:
That's a bad attitude.

Second Zombie:
I'm a zombie. What kind
of attitude do you expect
from a useless cog of rotting flesh?
Should I pretend that exercise
and diet will keep me alive forever?

First Zombie:
A little—hey, it's nice
to see you—wouldn't hurt.

Second Zombie: It's not nice to see you.
You look like dirt.
I don't even want to know
what I look like.
Who raised us from the dead
this time?

First Zombie:
Jesus, of course.

Second Zombie:
I know it was Jesus,
you dickless decaying zombie.
It's always Jesus.
I mean which Jesus this time?
The Statue of Liberty give me
your tired, your poor Jesus
or the good ol' gun-totin',
ass-kickin' Jesus.

First Zombie:
I'm pretty sure this Jesus
is our kind of Jesus,
the American Jesus

ready for barbecue and beer.
I'm pretty sure even you
would have voted for this Jesus.
Second Zombie:
I don't like any Jesus at all,
but as long as it's no
holier than thou rainbow coalition Jesus,
no urban fancy slick boy Jesus
I guess I'll do what I'm asked.
I want a job I can do
and someone who believes in America.
It's simple for me.
Otherwise, the whole country will be stormed
by people from who knows where.

Third Zombie: (limps up, sycophantic)
Hey, boys! What's happening?
I just took my Longeva
and when I woke up whammo.
No logic I can trust, only emotions
and really bad breath.
Looks like it's time
to slurp up some libtard brains
instead of listening to them whine
about snowflakes and unicorns.
I really miss the good old days
of taking out desperate poor people
in muddy hell holes
to fatten the American banking system.

Second Zombie:
The American banking system
went overseas and left me
with nothing. How do you think
I got dead in the first place?
(shakes head, disgusted)
Why, when Jesus
asks for zombies, does he give us

these shit for brains leaders
who line their own pockets?
Guess that's what
I deserve working 20 years
at the ampm in Kingston, Arizona.

First Zombie:
We've got a duty here all right?
I sure do love when I have a duty,
something to do with friends I trust.
So are we working together on this
or going to turn on each other
like a bunch of university communists?

Second Zombie:
I already said I was in.
What do you want me to do,
like it that I'm the guy that Jesus
uses to clean up his messes?

Third Zombie:
It's just like the old days
when men were men I could adore.
Now, I'm a zombie with a mission!
Brains, must eat brains!

First Zombie:
Brains, must eat brains!

end scene

Act 3, Scene 4: Jesus provides dispensations for devotees

(Painting of Papal dispensations maybe Titian or Tintoretto)
Five characters: Jesus (3), Minister (2), Lobbyist (5), CEO (1), Angel Raphael (4)

Jesus:
I'm glad to see the true followers are with me.
Minister, Lobbyist, CEO: (singing the Bryan Adams song with upstretched arms to Jesus)
"(Everything I do) I do It For You"

Jesus:
I know you would.
And soon you'll know
what you can do for me.
But now let's discuss
what I can do for you.
Line up, folks. Get your hands out.
What do you want? Ask for anything.
(All three stare at him)

Lobbyist:
Anything?

Jesus:
Yes.

Lobbyist:
Anything anything? Or just anything?

Jesus:
Ah. Yes. Anything anything.
(Note: Each character in the room is then going ask for what they want and this Jesus will say that he's giving it, although he has no power, actually, to do it)

Minister:
I'd like a chain of megachurches
in downtown Tulsa, Jackson,
Charlotte and Nashville.
Jesus:
Of course.
Your ministry is valuable to us
in these final days. We need to support

Raphael up here in heaven.
But that can't be all? Anything anything.
Minister: (grins)
Well. If you put it that way,
I would like an unbeliever
brought to me every day.
And a new sports car, every day.
And I want to drive that sports car
right into that unbeliever,
and I want it to be televised
and I want to get in no trouble at all.
How about that? And maybe for variation,
I want to gun some of them down
right on 5th Avenue while everyone cheers.

Jesus:
It shall be so. (turns to Lobbyist)
And you?

Lobbyist:
I want dessert every day for lunch and dinner.
I want servants lined up at my door.
I want the raiment of the Pope.
And I want no regrets.

Jesus:
Your loyalty will be rewarded.
And no regrets, dear boy. And?

Lobbyist:
And?

Jesus:
Yes.

Lobbyist:
Okay. I want to be a movie star.
I want to do sex scenes, real ones.

And I want a poster of me, naked,
to be the most popular poster in America,
and I want that poster in every bedroom in America,
and I want women and men, lots of them,
to see that poster when they're in a bedroom
with a man and I want them to wish, and say they wish,
that I was there, and that they feel disappointed
that I'm not. And I want no one, ever,
to ever remember Burt Reynolds or Lana Turner again.
(he looks around, embarrassed) Too much?
I knew it would be too much.

Jesus:
Not at all.

Lobbyist:
It's not too much?

Jesus:
It's already done. (turns to CEO)
You?

CEO:
We need to reorganize this place.
Heaven has too flat a pecking order.
I will report directly to the big guy.
My retinue should include both Raphael and Michael.
And of course I support Raphael
in his reorg according to your love
of profits, er, prophecy.

Jesus: (frowning)
Anything anything on Earth.

CEO:
You didn't say on Earth.

Jesus: (eyeing the CEO coldly)
Are you moving in on my territory?
Who do you think you are, Putin?
I know Putin. And let me tell you:
you're no Putin.

CEO:
You didn't say on Earth.

Jesus:
I did say on Earth. Are you calling me a liar?
I know you wouldn't. So, anything on Earth.
Don't hold back.

CEO:
But I didn't hold back.
Jesus: It's okay. Everybody holds back.

CEO: (adamant)
I want a piece of heaven. A big one.
Anything short of that, no dice.
Jesus: (snaps fingers) It's done.

CEO:
How so?

Jesus:
You're now 30% owner of heaven (™).
30% of proceeds from any business
using the word "heaven"
in any aspect of what it does
now belongs to you.

CEO:
That's not what I meant.

Jesus:
It is what you meant. So, what?

Nobody's got a song for Jesus? (and Minister and Lobbyist break into Bryan Adams' song: "(Everything I Do) I Do It For You")

CEO:
Hey.

Jesus:
Look. I'm the biggest, ever.
I'm bigger than biggest.
But I like your style.
Let's confer with some of these angels,
see if we can bring you in
on organizing heaven.
What about Attorney General?

CEO:
Attorney General of Heaven? I'd take
Attorney General of Heaven.

Raphael: (to Jesus)
I don't know if we can get that done.
(to himself) And what's in it for me?
Maybe I want to be Attorney General.
Or maybe just Secretary of Heaven's Interior.

Jesus:
If I ask you to do it, you'll do it.
Loyalty, that's what counts in heaven.
So, how's everybody feeling?

Minister, Lobbyist, and CEO:
"Everything I do / I do it for you"

Jesus:
And you should.
I've done more for humanity than anyone.
I'm, like, a smart person.

I love people and I do everything for you
and I do it really well.
Look at all those paintings of me,
even as an infant everybody loved me.
My mother loved me so much, I was amazing.
And I'm the most convincing speaker.
I can deal with a bad situation really well.

Minister, Lobbyist and CEO:
"Everything I do, I do for you"
(organ music, fade to black)

end scene

Act 4, Scene 4: Raphael and Michael plan to overthrow God

(Painting of Brutus and Cassius by Edward Loomis Davenport)
Two characters: Angel Raphael (4), Angel Michael (3)

Angel Raphael:
I know I've made mistakes.
Helping others is confusing.
But you betrayed my deal
With our charming corporates.
My new wings lost, I must
cope with tattered pinions.

Angel Michael:
I'm zealous and bloody, a purist,
I admit it,
but in this critical time
it doesn't serve
for every small offense
to cause rebuke.
Angel Raphael:
You protect the state of heaven

against intruders and transgression.
We honor you for that.
But now with Jesus gone
and too much power
in too few hands
God seizes more power
and sheds red blood
in our blue white eyrie.
Angel Michael:
You'd blame God
for your itchy palm?
As much as I reject
God taking all into his hands,
I cannot forget
your acquiescence to the CEO
and co-conspirators.

Angel Raphael:
I'm not the only player here.
All those corporate shills
that Jesus raised have turned
God to a vengeful version
of his former self, as if humanity
were still a tribe of unschooled herders. The Rapture 70

Angel Michael:
Such rough behavior does not train
our heavenly host to act
the way we claim we like them.
God's not much of a role model lately.

Angel Raphael:
Thank you for confirming
my suspicion. Look!
God's a fake.
He admits as much.
He's jealous and composed
of our fragments.

Let's get rid of him
and let the workers into paradise.
Angel Michael:
Are you sure they know
what to do with power?
Every time revolution wins
another set of oligarchs takes over.
The mass wreaks too much havoc
on itself for delicate decisions,
even those you know are good.

Angel Raphael:
They can't do worse.
The Earth is about to implode.
Toxicity and fire vent
into the very air they breathe.
Their skins are ashen
and their eyes flood.
We've got a big investment
in it. Knowing what will happen,
we let it happen anyway
to have our way, confirming
or should I say pretending
that our will impels our purpose.

Angel Michael:
I fear I may renounce my vows
and as a thing I myself am suspect—
as are you.

Angel Raphael:
That's the normal condition.
Don't follow me if
you think we only line our nest.
But if you believe, based on history
and faith, that when
the system stinks, cutting rot away
even to the bone

allows the whole to regain
its former glory, then we have to fight
and not only for ourselves.

Angel Michael:
OK. Let's shake it up
and let the chips land
where they may because
we know that once the riot
starts, control flies from our hands.

Angel Raphael:
But what do we do when that CEO and lobbyist
come storming in here
demanding their dessert?

Angel Michael:
One problem at a time, okay?
We've got to take on God directly
and go on from there.

Angel Raphael:
I sure am ready
to give God
a piece of my mind.

end scene

Epilogue: 'indeterminate purpose'

Image: Epilogue
One character: Mother (5)

Mother:
Thank you for your kind attention,
we know you've many grievances.
Our scenes spoke to morality
Through an unlikely sequence.
Power in the hands of few
that builds networks for all
depends on skills and strategies
that do the people's will.
We understand you've taken your seats
with certain prior allegiance.
You judge us based on what you think
already, in spite of new ideas and frequence.
The things we are are hardly fixed
But combined from their relations.
You love what you love in any case
In spite of our orations.
Protect what you are no matter what.
Never change your bold creations.
Ethics built in different frames
Can replace the morals of nations.

END play

Selfie: Poetry, Social Change & Ecological Connection

2016-2022

NETWORKS OF METAPHOR

> *. . . The U.S.-Mexican border es una herida abierta [an open wound] where the Third World grates against the first and bleeds. And before a scab forms, it hemorrhages again, the lifeblood of two worlds merging to form a third country—a border culture*
>
> —Gloria Anzaldúa

While Gloria Anzaldúa focuses on the suffering of border culture, I point to it as simultaneously a fertile area of change and responsive interaction. Standing in the way of implementing environmental models of culture that support change, inland humanism and the laws of nations depend on reinforcing the separation of me from everyone else.

. . . .

Borders are broader,
edges are entries,
margins marginalize and connect with page numbers,
limits limited range and shorter paths strengthen connections,
property lines align and conform.
Let the sets presently reset assumptions
how nouns and verbs proliferate
without telling us what to do with them.
How to engage more specific speech
as inhibition approaching borderlands?
How may I address you?....

. . . .

Frame borders as things with width,
depth, height, and extension over time,
the border's borders even.
What's going on in
that space between
that can ally us?
Prose becomes poetry
then reverts to it:

Borderlands
swell from one-dimensional lines

through the compound model of
things including molecules,
nouns, individuals, nations, concepts,
ecosystems. When we say
our organism exists, can we say
so for all parts or only when they
come together in the known
identity individuals construct
of things and selves? Scale
falters in perception
persisting. Borders expand
through thinking about them.
A person can be said
to exist, even described in parts,
and may be conscious. But is
my arm conscious? An octopus
may be said to be conscious, and,
per Smith, there is a greater likelihood
of extending consciousness
to its arms through its distributed
nervous system, distributed network, populations.2
My brain is dark
inside my skull, but connections
fill me with light.

....

The material and multiple connections that comprise environmental borders are as multidimensional as the vaunted interiors of minds in modernism. Rather than trying to invent a generalization or definition of borderlands, here are some exemplary ways to look at them. Some of these connections are explanatory, some are conceptual, some communicate the border crossing through poetic indirection:

1. Connections across borderlands may be point to point like whispering a poem in your ear (material being moving air), distributed over several channels at once like social media (material being electrical energy across a wire), and broadcast like cellular technology (material being microwaves) and solar radiation (material being the radiation).

2. How amazing that text connects.
I missed that scaled 与, that fish
who escapt the lure. Twice!
Slipt in votes fer them,
suppressing ballots of Browns.
Yes and so one is
writing in two directions at once.

3. The palpable, measurable border between my hand touching yours. Its heat, touch, run up the arm, focus the eyes, open the connecting capillaries, supporting connections to biology, law, sex, and signs.

4. A taste you suffer
Where th flame ends
Variations tho still one.
Differences linkt thru assonance,
rhyme, those different words, drowning
like Gerard Manley Hopkins' "six coiffed sisters" in
setting, prosody, logic, and page.

5. The many layers of skin (three major, multiple minor), blood vessels, nerves, hair, fat, integument. I kiss your cheek covered with bacteria. My lips splash through layers of increasing temperature, denser pheromones, resistance by your mind even when you want that kiss on your cheek.

6. The Seine River where sunlight ends
No, look, it sets here, too!

7. The border between El Paso and Ciudad Juarez changes thickness with changes in political administration. People, freight, and ideas (less, then more) continue to flow across the border. Poetic border crossing and overlapping ecological border counter the political border line reinforced by a new wave of white selfhood.

8. Oppression of the Other
pushes strongly in one direction.
Responses to oppression—
connection in Black communities,

assertion of southern lands,
monolithic feminism and queerness,
submission, questioning
dialectic, acknowledging
universal disability, asserted
consciousness, multiplicity—
contradict a singular view of self,
society and planet

9. The indirect connections of
a reference made to a friend
about what you did.
To whom. The words were
spoken and difficult
to retract since the words
are material, remembered, archived

10. Between I. A. Richards' "tenor and vehicle," between George Lakoff's "source and target" connectors carry thrown light, black dogs, etherized patients, and world stages between sectors of the brain and words of the text

11. Characters in novels
speaking to each
other on lawns

12. The soil allows us to attach ourselves and our plants while the world, too much with us, provokes detachment. Attachments evaporate the illusion of a great being outside. Detachment helps us escape the delusion of borderline.

13. "A dark green raincoat she ran into" (Zhao Si)
Pouring a glass of water overwhelms the lip.

14. Fruit flies dance out our door.
I catch you saying that again,
again you must be somewhere to mean it.
A selfie shows what
was behind you and around.

15. The intermittent but regular
connections of taxmen reach,
the toll taker receives,
collection plate passes,
the date waits for you
to take or not to take a pill.
Many to many

16. Connection breaches the personal/social
boundary linking many to many

17. Is there any connection
between a screen loading
and recall? Is there any?
Shape to it!

18. The strong connections of motherhood,
the weaker yet still material connections of fatherhood, the connections of love,
clearly material and based on fluid
exchange, chattel and use value, the different
connections of friendship supported by various roles
such as long relationships, jobs
and interests, friendships:
enjambment due to other friendships

19. Divine destination in your eyes
Somewhere I, we, they: the heavenly host-
ess cupcakes, hoping not to be toppled
by twinkies.

20. The model links characters in theater, actors on political stages and ghosts that haunt our demonstrable things and those that exist most strongly in language and sensibility, the connections across lines of thought that science proves and those it doesn't validate.

21. How far do I have
to go to get to

where you are
so we can be here?

22. The strong connections of a Black man to the daily pain and pride of his color. The characteristics of that connection—job performance, family stability, class connections—when pain bleeds into self-doubt, what is spoken about as color. The resilience against pain fashioned by community…

23. Driven by dread of distinction
"However the image enters" (Audre Lorde)
  "The perversity
   of separation, isolation," (Amiri Baraka)
"An intensely slanted approach…" (Edward Bland)

24. We Jews learned our lesson. Shepherds, slaves, then millennia of separation from Christian societies where my ancestors lived. Trying to connect through borders in Europe, we joined the elite and the working classes. Separation reasserts itself in holocaust, six million dead and Jews flee to Palestine, the US, Argentina. Now Israel reproduces that ghetto wall against attacks from Palestinians whose name the land bears. The wall ignores citizenship, familial ties, human rights to protect individual, threatened, Jewish bodies, corporate productivity, and the corpse of the state. Reconnect despite the risks of threats to life and tribe.

25. A baby-boom generation protecting truth at all costs
engenders a generation intent on no harm at all costs.

26. The connections of youth to age, anger to fear,
power to privilege, sex to love that
reiterate binary identity!

27. Beauty connected to arbitrary choices, &
to patterns of calcium propagation, &
to realms of mathematical possibility, &
to economics by our willingness to write
through activation and inhibition signals
through air, through mind, with light, in random

placement of color on her feathers,
as in poetry we inhibit grammar
through connectors to politics,
deleting "the",
to metric apostrophes,
to prosody adding through which
readers awake their aware.

28. I wrote a personal poem through me
a social poem through them
an eco-poem through us
connecting through a fourth line.

29. Bi-directional connections of gender.
A sport teems. How strongly
class distinctions and daily
activities determine and
reestablish connections
to build a social network,
flexible borderlands.

30. Your self is not a unit of one;
Multidirectional writing: that's the whole poem,
because any word could appear next.
It's just a fact of writing
and if you object that a perfect wor(l)d
should appear next or some synonym
then you haven't been paying attention.

31. The intermittent connections to corporate identity reinforced by marketing, advertising, and public relations. Leaders seek to create connections between workers and management while severing connections between workers that strengthen their communities. Supply chains imitate family ties and forest ecology, as well as slave trade routes. (Stefano Harney & Fred Moten)

32. Corporate identity links consumers and suppliers of product to the corporate body that acts like an organism, acts like a city, acts like a mind. (Marsilius of Padua) But cities are harder to kill.

33. Connections are nouns
made up of components
an over populated dmz
to make want disappear
and create desire
like all things connected
and simultaneously separate,
a characteristic of language.

34. "I don't remember." (Cure)
Obsessive productivity
recapitulates the self.

35. The connections across boundaries between one poem and another both of which I wrote. The connections and borderlands between poems I wrote and those you wrote. The connections and social borderlands between a poet and a group of poets, casual and formal, connections across social boundaries between poets and a group of non-poets, walls between poets and markets, connections and walls (borderlands) between poetry and society, connections made here between poetry and the biosphere, what I'm writing here and speaking now connecting to you!

36. Multiple uses of the same thing,
pliers to open and close,
tie otherwise diverse
functions out there in the field
and inside in the head together:
enjambment as a mental connection

37. Links don't just exist at the edges of entities. Many begin from the core function of an individual's love, family, blood flow, property, and poetry. Interior-to-interior connections are as crucial to the organism than those beginning at the edges of entities because every organism is composed of many linked parts. More connections within the organism than between organisms help define its identity.

38. One more poem here!
If you write it, then

we're a thing, the
enjambment of sex.

39. These are my personal boundaries
Do not cross them…

40. Some things are connected and function together like a fork and spaghetti. Some appear to be connected by being in a related category, but the connection is not functional like a fork and a banana. Some things might be functionally related but are not usually used at the same time like a claw hammer and a sledge hammer. Some things are functionally unrelated and don't appear together like a kangaroo and a hammer. Some things are functionally unrelated but have other relations like a giraffe and a pencil: remember connections to the glass of water.

41. Breaking and entering
into the paradise of me,
suffering in my domain,
reminding the preacher that
life is surplus energy
that founds
&&& causes warming.
Why do I want to sustain
that image, that paradise
of glass that poetry

Borderlands composed this way become porous and permeable, scary to the highly defended self. They are difficult to contemplate as a unit since they are composites of diverse connections, diverse characteristics. Yet they are a commonplace unnoticed.

The poet sees this coming and protects their lyric.

. . . .

Acknowledgments

Lazy Sonnets was published by Potes & Poets Press, 1976. Editor Peter Ganick.

Part Songs was published by Roof Books, 1978. Editor Brita Bergland.

In Case was published by Sun & Moon Press, 1981. Editor Douglas Messerli.

Converses was published by Awede Press, 1982. Editor Brita Bergland.

Popular Fiction was published by Roof Books, 1985. Editor James Sherry.

The Word I Like White Paint Considered was published by Awede Press, 1986. Editor Brita Bergland.

Our Nuclear Heritage was published by Sun & Moon Press, 1991. Editor Douglas Messerli.

Four For was published by Meow Press, 1995. Editor Joel Kuszai.

OOPS! was published by Blaze Vox [Books], 2013. Editor Geoffrey Gatza.

Entangled Bank was published by Chax, 2016. Editor Charles Alexander.

The Oligarch was published by Palgrave Macmillan, 2018. Thanks to Jacob Dreyer.

The Rapture, a collaborative play written with Mark Wallace, was produced online and at the 300 Bowery Segue loft during the Covid pandemic. Produced by Lonely Christopher's Inter Poets Theater. Thanks too to the actors for both productions.

Selfie: Poetry, Social Change & Ecological Connection was published by Palgrave Macmillan, 2022. Thanks to Jacob Dreyer.

James Sherry is the author of 14 books of poetry and prose, most recently *Selfie: Poetry, Social Change & Ecological Connection* (Palgrave MacMillan, 2022) and the poetry book *Entangled Bank* (Chax Press, 2016). Since 1976, he has edited Roof Books and Roof Magazine, publishing nearly 200 titles of seminal works of language writing, flarf, conceptual poetry, new narrative, and environmental poetry. He started The Segue Foundation, Inc. in 1977, producing over 10,000 events of poetry and other arts in NYC.

For more, see jamessherry.net.

Designed by Charles Alexander for Chax Press.

Albertina type font has been used throughout.

Thanks to Cynthia Miller for her art work on the cover and for her ongoing support of Chax Press.